The Pursuit:

A Meditation on Happiness

Also by Gerry LaFemina:

Prose Poems

Notes for the Novice Ventriloquist
Figures from The Big Time Circus Book/The Book of Clown Baby
Zarathustre in Love
Baby Steps in Doomsday Prepping

Poems

The Story of Ash
Little Heretic
Vanishing Horizon
The Parakeets of Brooklyn
The Window Facing Winter
Graffiti Heart
Voice, Lock, Puppet: Poems of Ali Yuce. Trans/ with Sinan Toprak
Shattered Hours: Poems 1988-1994
23 Below

Fiction

Clamor.
Wish List: Stories

Criticism

Composing Poetry: A Guide to Writing Poems and Thinking Lyrically
Palpable Magic: Essays on Poets and Prosody

The Pursuit:
A Meditation on Happiness

Gerry LaFemina

Lake Dallas, Texas

Cover Design: Jacqueline Davis
Cover Art: "Untitled" by Cliff Wockenfuss/Zito Art, Pittsburgh
Author Photo: Mercedes Hettich

ISBN: 978-1-948692-78-6 Paper, 978-1-948692-79-3 ebook
Library of Congress Control Number: 2021940750

For Brandon Fury
For Kara Knickerbocker

And for Mercedes Hettich

America is a vast conspiracy to make you happy.
— John Updike

Happiness is not an ideal of reason, but of imagination.
— Immanuel Kant

To be without some of the things you want is an indispensable part of happiness.
— Bertrand Russell

Author's note: The following takes place on January 4, 2018 from 7:00 to 11:00 pm

THE STANFORD ENCYCLOPEDIA OF PHILOSOPHY BEGINS ITS ENTRY ON HAPPINESS this way: "What is happiness? This question has no straightforward answer, because the meaning of the question itself is unclear. What exactly is being asked?"

Seems as good a place to start as any. Or to riff on Raymond Carver, as many writers will, this book might be called "What We Talk about When We Talk about Happiness." Another look at *The Stanford Encyclopedia* suggests that we think of happiness in one of two ways, as either a state of mind, or as a life that goes well for the person living it.

Perhaps like light it is simultaneously a wave and particle, both are true, at least in how we conceive it in the West, in the fast-moving twenty-first century. We live in a time when technology makes our lives easier and yet people seem unhappier. By "unhappier," what do I mean? Less fulfilled, perhaps? More despairing? Technology gives us more leisure time, but we seem to be toiling more: checking work emails on vacation or taking care of some correspondence at home. We often spend leisure time on the Internet. Social media makes it easier to compare our lives with the "lives" of others (and by that, I mean what they willingly and publicly display for others), and those of us who spend any time on social media have seen a link to an article detailing how time spent on Facebook and Instagram make us less happy in that it leads us to compare how our lives compare with the perceived lives of others. Among the writer friends I know, I often hear complaints about the number of rejections they've received while they see posts detailing their friends' acceptance letters and publications. It makes no difference that these writers who complain know that few people post about the twenty-some-odd rejection letters they've recently received. Despair and joy are not bound by what we know. They are mental and neurological activities, surely, having to do with dopamine receptors, et cetera, none of which have to do with the intellectual neurological aspects of brain function.

Note well: I am not a brain scientist. I am not a philosopher (though I was a philosophy major!). I am not, probably, all that qualified to talk about "happiness" because I may not be happy in many ways that people like to think about it. I've felt, even recently, great envy, frustration, grief, loneliness and more of what we would call the sadder emotions, but I will say, too, without qualification that I am happy.

Mostly.

PEOPLE WHO KNOW ME—AND BY THAT, I MEAN PEOPLE WHO MAY EVEN BE, socially, my friend—consider me a happy person. They may think other things of me—I'm sure some think I'm arrogant or insecure or even somewhat of an asshole, and I have no doubt that I can come off as each of these things (and plenty of other things, too) at times. Since this is not a study called "On 'Arrogance'" or "On 'Assholiness'," my focus will remain on the numerous times I've been told by acquaintances from various parts of my life that they think of me as "happy." By this, I think they mean that I enact certain social graces we associate with "happiness": I'm gregarious, quick to tell a joke or story, generous, sympathetic. I smile. I practice compassion. I tease myself and others though I pay attention to not cross a line: I try to use discretion and not tease somebody who is hurting. Most importantly to this outward sense of happiness is that I laugh. Often and out loud and without embarrassment. In general, I enact the learned behavior associated with *joi de vivre*.

In the United States, we are obsessed with happiness. According to the most recent World Happiness Report (2017), the U.S. population has experienced a reduced sense of happiness, dropping from third to nineteenth in the last ten years. No wonder there's an industry of self-help books and billion-dollar pharmaceutical businesses designed to lesson our pain, our depression, our anxiety. A side show of doctors has set up tents on television; they gladly tell us their secrets to being happy: they must be happy themselves, the way they smile with some smug assuredness that has everything to do with having a producer, a director, a makeup artist, a sponsor. Do what you love, they say. Look out for number one. Be mindful. Find god. Take a pill. Have one glass of wine a day. Join a 12-step program, a self-help group, a bowling league. Do what it takes…

We have the right to pursue happiness. It's right there in the constitution, after the rights of life and liberty. That doesn't mean we have the right to happiness, just the right to pursue it.

It's interesting language, isn't it? *The right to **pursue** happiness*, as if it were a rabbit to be tracked and trapped. We are Elmer Fudd after the wascally wabbit, heh heh heh heh heh. And like Bugs Bunny, it always seems to elude us. I don't know how many times I got what I thought would bring me happiness, only to have the rifle blast backfire.

L IKE SO MANY THINGS IT STARTS AT A YOUNG AGE, OUR SENSE OF HAPPINESS, our beliefs in what will "make" us happy. When I look back, I can think of many things that added to my joy. See above: Looney Toons. Also, I enjoyed riding my used Huffy and feeling cool air in my hair, my cheeks flush with October wind. I enjoyed playing with Lego and with this Evel Knievel doll that rode a stunt motorcycle: I'd put him on the bike, the bike on its charger, and then turn the crank till the motorcycle zoomed off. I'd build ramps from game boards for Evel to get airborne. Sometimes imitating the daredevil on that Huffy is what did it. After a day of such play, I would lay each night in my mother's bed and read beside her, glad she was home, finally, from work. She would read, too, and that sense of quiet togetherness filled an hour of my days with a little less loneliness, less anxiety about her absence. When she wasn't home, I laughed at cartoons or reruns of *I Love Lucy* and *Happy Days*. Like all children, I knew how to laugh.

Ditto, like all children I knew how to cry. My father wouldn't show up to take my brother and sister and me out on his required Sundays, off, no doubt, playing cards in the Brooklyn "club" where the Italian men smoked and ante-ed, and raised the pot because they were holding an eight-high straight. Left waiting, not yet used to such disappointment as I was the youngest by seven years, I would feel sad. Once, I got home from school and the door to the apartment had been jimmied, something was jammed into the keyhole, and I had to stay across the street with Tommy Tierney and his family, call my mother. I spent the rest of the semester scared of a break in. When I was nine, two twenty-year-old neighborhood guys chased me down, pulled me into the tall weeds beside the Staten Island Rapid Transit line and forced me, at knife point, to give them both blow jobs. I didn't even know the term for what I had to do. It was late summer, maybe a week or so before school would start. This was the 1970s, the City near bankruptcy. No one maintained this strip of land. The weeds were brown, tall as corn stalks: they were a great place to hide out for a few hours. We younger kids would go and tell dirty jokes and trade comic books, always leaving before dark. We'd see the remains of the older kids' nights there: beer bottles, cigarette butts.

I remember being chased down: I couldn't pedal my beat-up bike fast enough. They dragged to that place that had been a not-so-secret escape, the Huffy slumped by the street. After that day I never went back. What was I to do right then, the knife blade there by my cheek. I got down on my knees, shaking. I lived with shame for decades.

Despite this pain, I remained able to play, splashing in the Tierneys' pool the rest of summer. Sometimes. Laugh as I might, swim as my might, I could never rinse the stain of that time from me.

BUDDHISM TEACHES NON-DUALITY. THERE IS NO EITHER/OR IN BUDDHIST philosophy. My grammar school years were a combination of sadness, violence, freedom, wonder, failure, heartache, success, and exuberance. In that regard they were, indubitably, like many other childhoods. These things can not be separated; they are inherently bound together not in the double helix of my DNA, but held, as much as my organs are, in the shell of this body. Which of these experiences do I own, and which do I let own me? So long ago, now, they exist nowhere else other than inside me.

Once, years ago, when I first started writing about being molested, the husband of a woman in my MFA program spoke with me after a reading and said he was sorry for what had occurred that day in Staten Island. "Sorry" such a strange word: it's both an apology and a statement of sympathy mixed with pity. Since I knew he didn't mean it as an apology, I was perplexed by his sentiment. What had happened happened: it can't be undone. It has led to me being the person I am. In relationships I do not tend to be the assertive one sexually. It has led me to be a careful listener to those who have been the victims of abuse. I don't know who I would be without that event in my life, and I have no desire to be someone else.

That's not to say it was easy. For years I was shy around women, uncertain how to ask someone out on a date, torn between physical desire and emotional turmoil. I did not know how to risk rejection, and I hated how I looked. I often felt not good-enough. This is a familiar legacy of shame: what had happened to me must somehow be my fault, and it played out in a variety of insecurities.

This may seem ironic because many people think of me as a flirt. And I am. It's a kind of compensation. Despite what happened, I think the human species, in general, as genuinely good-hearted. I like people, I like the interaction and back and forth of flirting. It's a kind of social commerce, one meant not to demean or to prey; it is meant to share a pleasantry. I have no problem telling someone, male or female, that they look good today. Why shouldn't someone be complimented for how they put themselves together. As a child, I often didn't look good: I had ill-fitting clothes, often hand me downs, and no one taught me how to groom. The molestation made it worse. To be told I looked good when I was a teenager and young adult gave me a rush of that satisfied the ego. Sometimes, it still does. Why wouldn't I want someone else to have such a moment?

That said, I don't flirt indiscriminately, and I don't flirt with an intention beyond the moment of flirtation, the moment of sharing a superficial but real pleasure. If one can flirt with mindfulness, I try to. If someone tells me they prefer not to be told such things, if they don't respond in kind, I apologize. I don't do it again. Respecting someone's space is part of their happiness. Respecting it also contributes to my own.

ONE OF THE KEY COMPONENTS OF SHAME IS HOW IT ISOLATES US. As with many of the negative emotions, we bear guilt and shame alone. It inherently makes us outside of the community, often because what shames us is against cultural norms. Is it any wonder so many ancient punishments were banishments: think Oedipus wandering, blindly, in his final days. He can't even see the outside world and thus is left to look inwardly, at his horror. How terrible he must look to those who see him.

Maybe that's the importance of Yom Kippur or the act of taking penance. The releasing of shame and guilt for our sins by giving voice to them is supposed to liberate us from our metaphoric banishments. But being a victim can bring shame without the act of sinning, and there's no ritual for the release of such a feeling. We bear it. I bore it for years. I was aware I didn't fit in because of it, and so I rejected standards. Mohawk. Combat boots. Black leather jacket. Machine gun drums and chain saw guitars. The punk community included many outcasts, an Island of Misfit Toys. Unfortunately, on Staten Island in 1983, there weren't many punks. I was a misfit toy without an island.

Of course, this dress didn't go unnoticed. As an adolescent in the 80s, some of the common taunts by guys gave witness to their own homophobia: *faggot* and *homo*. It was used on the ball courts and written in bathroom stalls: _____*is gay;* it was called out in the cafeteria and spat out when a hand might push me on the chest at the bus stop. I didn't fit in, and if I didn't fit in in ways my schoolmates didn't understand, then they would make an accusation of not fitting in that they did understand. So often, what we think of as slurs is more often than not a reaffirmation of someone else's fear. To use such language is to admit the weakness of their own standing.

As a young punk, I read *the Village Voice* each week in part to find out what bands were playing where; the other students in my school knew little of punk rock or Manhattan. For them Greenwich Village was New York's gay neighborhood, and if I read the *Village Voice,* I must be gay. I heard the word *faggot* a lot. I was a straight guy ashamed of having been molested by two men and because of that I was also awkward around girls, incapable of participating in the bravado teen guy rituals of assertive desire.

I spent a lot of time self-isolating.

ISOLATION IS NOT ABOUT INDIVIDUALITY. ISOLATION IS A WAY OF SUFFERING. Crusoe on his island feels miserable until he finds Friday. NASA worries about the effect of being alone in space without community when thinking about manned interplanetary missions. Solitary confinement is one of the harshest punishments of our criminal justice system. People trapped in cycles of shame, of guilt, often spend more time looking inwardly instead of at their community. They believe no one will understand. Oedipus is vulnerable in his isolation and blindness, both real and metaphoric. Imagine him, hand flailing in front of him, knowing what he's done and believing everyone knows what he's done.

I spent much of my childhood alone: father gone, much older siblings with lives of their own, a mother who worked sometimes three jobs to ensure the bills got paid. But I was lucky: when my mother ran her errands, she took me with her, almost always. To the supermarket, to the cleaners, to pick up Avon, to the beauty parlor. I would pack some books with me to entertain myself, maybe one of those *Yes & Know* books with the yellow highlighter that revealed answers to trivia and puzzles, later a Mattel hand-held football or baseball game, but for those hours in the passenger seat of her car or walking together down the grocery store aisles, I wasn't alone. And even if I bore my shame with me, I was out in the community of adults, one that seemed so much less hateful than the community of peers.

THE SUITE I'M STAYING IN: LIVING ROOM, BEDROOM, KITCHEN, AND BATHROOM. I sit at a desk in the living room near the entrance to the hallway. The table is translucent acrylic; the chair designed to be comfortable-enough. Behind me on the far wall, the window shakes with winter. The walls are white like the snow lit by the courtyard lamps. The furniture is high end Ikea: serviceable, comfortable, attractive in that way that has little of its own personality. The same can be said for the wall art: the photograph of the large rubber ducky is particularly compelling insofar as it seems to watch me, the way the moose heads do in certain movies of the forties and fifties. Or perhaps the way god does for some people. It doesn't judge, necessarily, but it watches. It's aware.

It is nicer than some apartments I've lived in. Nicer than the cells where I've slept in meditation retreats where I'd hoped I'd find some peace or at least some understanding, and where I often did, only to forget to pack it with my luggage when I returned home. Nicer than the rooms at certain writers retreats where I'd written and read, and then socialized too much in the evenings, talking about art and sex and music and poetry, and listening to the lies, great and small, that happen in such moments.

I have decided tonight I will sit at the dining table when my dinner arrives. Too many dinners and even more lunches have I eaten at my desk, ignoring the taste of the food for the taste of the words I tried to craft, the pastiness of the paper. I had to learn to eat, to slow down, to recognize that savoring a meal is to be grateful for it. It's similar to why I often close my eyes when I go to readings: I want to focus on just the reader's voice, the words, their rhythms and sounds: I do not want to focus on the back of the head sitting in front of me. I've talked about this at writers retreats as well.

On another night, perhaps I'd be out with some of the other faculty or the students, but not tonight. It's frigid out. Everyone has writing to do. Or reading. Most likely both, and there's an advisory about being out too long in such temperatures. I am not particularly lonely or alone: the duck watches as I work. When the phone rings and it's my mother, I let it go to voice mail.

13

MY MOTHER TALKS TO STRANGERS; IT'S A TRAIT I'VE LEARNED FROM HER. Cashiers, taxi drivers, wait staff, people seated beside me on a plane, customers at the neighboring table: I've spoken to them all, often joking with them until all were smiling. The Dalai Lama talks about the importance of community, of social interaction, and being aware of its import. Such moments of positive interaction, even if it's just a *thank you* when holding a door for someone, now adds to my joy. Our inability to survive alone as children requires us to live in families, in communities, in villages. And although this can lead to a kind of tribalism and fear of other, it also emphasizes this need to exist in a world of people. We find comfort in our friends, in our families, in a group identity. Our capacity to live among others is key to our survival and to a sense of well-being.

It is for this reason I do not understand when Christians get upset about people wishing them a "Happy holiday," and how this has led to a claim that there is a war on Christmas. For that matter, I do not understand why others might get upset by being told "Merry Christmas," or "Happy Chanukah," or "Joyous Ramadan." The former is a statement of respect for others: it says, "I do not know if you celebrate, what you celebrate, or how you celebrate, but I want your celebrations to be happy." The other is a statement of respect for others: "In my tradition we say _____, and I want to share that spirit with you and yours whatever you celebrate." Whatever the expression, these statements are blessings for happiness, for merriness, for joyousness. Who could be upset about that? Or more to the point, why would anyone choose to be?

In many situations such as this one, being insulted is a choice. There's a big difference between a verbal attack—a slur, a deliberate attempt to inflict anguish—and a wish to be inclusive. There's a difference between the classmates who called me *faggot* and the cashier wishing someone else a *happy holiday*; still, we choose how we react. A

Buddhist monk once taught me that we can't control what others do, can only control how we respond.

What does a war on Christmas sound like? Surely, not "Happy holidays." If someone said "Fuck your Christmas," okay. That's a curse. But to be upset about a blessing of happiness, however it is expressed, is to reject a blessing. I reject no blessings.

Where does happiness start? I don't know, but I can say where it doesn't start. It does not start by looking for grievances, looking for slights. It does not start by looking at what you don't have, at who you aren't. If a stranger were to come up to us in the mall and give us a dollar, would we be insulted? What if it were two Euros? Or a Canadian loonie? Or would we say thank you with a bemused expression on our face? Our response is up to us.

May the Buddha smile upon you.

WHAT'S AMAZING ABOUT OUR CAPACITY TO FIND INSULTS IS HOW OFTEN what we perceive as a slight is about affiliation, about the cultures and subcultures we identify with. Most sports teams have rivals, and we treat the fans of those rivals as if they were the enemy. In politics these days, it's gotten worse. Those who declare there's a war on Christmas suggest that the insult of "happy holidays" is an attack on their religion. The inclusiveness of happy holidays seems to threaten the exclusive membership of Christianity, and some news outlets and talking heads make this an issue to help establish their affiliations. Those kids who called me *homo* saw this as excluding me from certain groups, emphasized the otherness my dress and music italicized.

Racial slurs do similar things: they emphasize otherness, they are designed to exclude by rejecting that otherness via derogatory language. These are the words of the majority, expressions of power used often by people whose own place in the world remains uncertain. Insults, in other words, are expressions of the uneasiness of the one casting the insult. That fact is happy people don't insult others; they have no need to hurt anyone. Let me repeat that: happy people have no need to insult others.

No doubt our arrival at school (and our first attempts at socializing), is where many of us learn insults and teasing; suddenly removed from an environment we know surrounded by people we know, we're among strangers. We seek safety of a familiar community and otherness feels threatening. This continues for years: adolescence is fraught with insecurity because our bodies change dramatically and our blood courses with added chemicals and hormones. So many stupid words come out of an adolescent's mouth, and today, social media allows for them to be caught on film in ways that do nobody a service.

As a child and teenager, I couldn't wait to be an adult: I dreamt of freedoms that I didn't realize would be hampered by bills and chores and obligations. The compromised workplace, the competition for jobs, the need to provide myself food and shelter never played into my dreams of adulthood despite watching my mother head off on Saturday mornings to a second job, transcribing dictation at St. Vincent's Hospital for years. Then later selling real estate. We believe in an American dream, in opportunity, in the possibility. Let's face it, when we dream of our future, we are more often than not dreaming of it without the strife we currently experience. How heartbreaking it is, then, when we are adults and jobs are scarce, our car breaks down, we decide to keep the heat on low in the winter and wear a sweater because we worry about the gas bill.

CONSIDER: NO ONE SAID "ALL LIVES MATTER" UNTIL SOMEONE SAID "Black lives matter." It became a rallying cry among many white Americans because suddenly they felt that their lives were being devalued; it was as if their security as a majority in this country, holding the majority of elected and official positions in this country was suddenly at risk.

The fact is, there's an unspoken "too" at the end of the phrase, "Black lives matter." It's implicit. It's a way of acknowledging a source of insecurity for an entire third of the United States population: since their arrival as chattel in the slave trade the lives of African Americans have mattered less to most Americans: slavery, Jim Crow laws, the fallacy of separate but equal. After having its first African American president (a president twice elected into office who had people claiming his presidency was illegitimate by branding him an "outsider") the country elected someone who pushed the birther conspiracy, railed against immigrants, and capitalized on mainstream fears about other marginalized groups (LBGTQ individuals, Muslims, Asians …).

The strategy of the Trump campaign (and of what I see of his presidency) isn't designed to improve the lives of white Americans so much as it is to reinforce their sense of security by reinforcing their separateness from other. This is much the same way that the Christian right uses the "war on Christmas." Surveys show, however, the white Americans, in general, have greater freedom, less insecurity, and overall, more happiness than people of other races. They live with more security, literally and figuratively. This only seems to suggest the precariousness of that security and the happiness that accompanies it.

HISTORICALLY, RACE BAITING HAS OFTEN BEEN USED AT TIMES WHEN WORK was scarce and financial stability shaken. We've seen it often: things have gone south and people sought a scapegoat. Immigrants are often the first decried for taking jobs away because they're outside the social framework: by color, by accent, by language, by religion. The fact that most decisions about who gets jobs are made by bosses not those hired don't factor into the response: often our bosses look and sound just like us. As a matter of fact, they have the success we dream about ourselves. More, in an increasingly technologized world, jobs are being taken away by automation, not immigration, but it's hard to hate a machine: so many machines have made our lives easier and cursing out a computer just gets a blinking cursor in response.

Similarly, in an increasingly secularized world, Christians are concerned about their standing: these cultural changes breed insecurity. They see immigrants who worship differently, who believe differently, and they're instincts are fear.

Yet what's so amazing is how Christianity teaches "love thy neighbor" and "do unto others as you would have done to you." In the tale of the Good Samaritan, members of the victim's tribe ignore the wounded man; it is only the other who helps. How did we get to the point of looking for hurt not love? I want to have a happy holiday. I want you to have one, too, whatever you celebrate.

KOOL & THE GANG'S "CELEBRATE" IS NOW IN MY HEAD. I'M SUBJECT TO earworms of all sorts. "Celebrate" is infectious: the funky bass, the synthesizer rhythm with its major chords, those horns. It's hard not to want to dance, to sing along, to, well, celebrate and have a good time (come on), for a little bit.

The holidays are a time of celebration, and despite the rumor that more people commit suicide from Thanksgiving through the New Year, the Annenberg Center for Public Policy shows the statistics don't match the myth. In fact, the suicide rates decline in these periods. The reasons are obvious, despite the stress, the commercial cajoling for us to spend money that we often don't have, the engaging with relatives and friends and coworkers in situations that make us uncomfortable, there's something good about celebrating,

Consider *A Christmas Carol:* Scrooge is miserable despite his money, his self-isolation adding to his misery. Bob Cratchett, on the other hand, is happy despite his son's health, his family's woeful financial states. He struggles but he is happy. He understands the importance of making merry. Happiness is about choosing to do what makes merry for you when you can. Cratchett might work long hours in miserable conditions for a surly miser, but it supplies him a means be happy outside work.

My mother used to take me on a day off to see the Christmas display windows at the Manhattan department stores even though we couldn't afford anything inside because the displays were startling: animatronic figures, lights, landscapes of fake snow and glitter that seemed almost other worldly and caused the viewer to wonder. Yearly, people drive for hours to see particularly decorated neighborhoods, the lights fighting off the early nights in the darkest days of the year in the northern hemisphere. That's what they're meant to do: fight the darkness, both externally and internally.

EACH AUTUMN, THE LARGE HOLIDAY CATALOGS FROM SEARS AND JC PENNEY would come in the mail, and also from Popular Club Plan, a mail-order goods company my mother would order Christmas presents from because they offered "points." As a kid I would go through these "wish books" circling the presents I hoped to get come December 25th. Sometimes things I'd seen on commercials were in the catalogs; sometimes they weren't, but I knew the majority of whatever Christmas loot I was getting would come from these books. I would return to them several times a week, the pages glossy as a dirty magazine.

We were economically strapped, but my mother was the daughter of Depression-era parents. She understood deprivation and going without, so each year she tried to make Christmas special. It didn't matter that my school uniform was often composed of hand-me-downs that Sister Jeanine, the school principal, collected. It didn't matter that another check bounced. It didn't matter that my mother washed clothes late, hung them to dry on basement lines, and if they weren't dry in time, she stuck them in a warm oven before the bus came. It didn't matter that there would be bills to pay come the new year. This was an opportunity to make her three children "happy" by fulfilling some wish book wishes. She tried hard to make sure there was an aura of specialness to it all, waiting till Christmas eve to wrap gifts, putting them out after we went to sleep, even when I was a teenager and my brother and sister were in their twenties.

The goal was to make something special, special. Even with her grandchildren she has continued to live with that philosophy. It's a good rule to live by. How important it is to make others feel special, and how empowering it is. Sometimes I forget this, complain about the gifts that seem over-the-top or inappropriate or wasteful, but in the end, she's saying "happy holidays."

THAT'S NOT TO SAY I DIDN'T WANT TO BE SOMEONE ELSE WHEN I WAS A CHILD. I longed to be as cool as Fonzie, as courageous as Captain Kirk, as good a pitcher as Tom Seaver, as daredevil as Evel Knievel, as debonair as James Bond, as smart as Sherlock Holmes, as rocking as Keith Richards. My role models were there on TV and in the movies and on the radio. They defined the positive attributes of popular culture, of masculinity, of what I (and many others) hoped to *be*. To be like these people would lead me to happiness, to overcoming the shame of my sadnesses, those hurts I carried that I thought no one else bore. Surely, none of my heroes did.

Whatever flaws these characters (real or fictional) had, were present but unexplored. Sure, Fonzie couldn't say "sorry" and, sure, he was a high school dropout, these were rarely explored as hindrances to Fonzie's happiness or cool (or the loneliness that led him to living above the Cunningham's garage and being adopted as part of the family). We never saw Evel Knievel with his multiple broken bones, addled on pain killers, barely able to walk. Holmes's opium use never seemed an issue to his capacity, and his arrogance was laughable: he was, after all, the smartest man in the books, why shouldn't he own it? Keef's drug problem wasn't the root of some unhappiness, just a by-product of counter-culture cool. Besides, we never saw him throwing up from heroin, shaking with the detox, nodding out.

That's the problem with media posturing; what's often shown is one side of the coin. Nonduality dictates there must be a second side, but we often aren't allowed to see it. This skews our understanding of the self.

For the record I didn't want to be Elmer Fudd. He seemed perpetually unhappy.

I N Jamaica they say 'the want for a thing is more than its worth.' I used to hear my former girlfriend's mother say that often, including about Shari's and my relationship. Wanting imbues the wanted with a kind of fetishistic value: how often did I see something I wanted and set about getting it only to be disappointed and to move on to the next wanting?

What I had to learn of course that wanting something comes with the responsibility of having it. Many parents with children who beg them for pets understand this: they see getting their child the wanted pet will teach the child responsibility. *Our daughter will walk the dog. Our son will feed the cat and clean out the boxes.* And what if the cat doesn't cuddle with the boy the way he'd hoped. What if the dog doesn't want to play fetch? The cat does what the cat does. The dog does what the dog does: the son, the daughter, still has to take care of the pet.

As a child in the seventies, I would often see a little convertible roadster, be it a Fiat, or a Triumph, or an MG, and I would want it. They were sporty, zippy, and uncommon. When I had the opportunity in my mid-twenties during a cancer scare to buy an MGB I saw in a field, I jumped on it. I had wanted one for two decades, after all. I was a city boy who'd known how to change a tire and change the oil of a car and had driven a manual transmission only a handful of times. Owning the car would require work: I'd have to learn to take care of it. To want something in the moment is often to ignore what the having entails. It can lead to a cycle of disappointment and more want.

As I write this, I'm in a hotel thinking about options for dinner. Often when I'm in a major city, I like to get cuisines that I can't get in the small Western Maryland town where I live. Although there's a great Caribbean restaurant in town, tonight I have settled on Indian food, and I'm excited to see goat on the menu. Because of the weather, I'm ordering in. I would like to use a promo code for the meal, but despite my attempts to input different codes found online, none of them seem to work. I can feel the agitation rising: I am already spending a lot of money, why wouldn't I want to save a few dollars. I fear, though, the agitation will mean I will not enjoy the meal, and so finally after the seventh coupon code fails to get my discount I give up and order the take out. Even though I've stepped up a few levels to be firmly lodged in the middle class but not so far up that I can be a spendthrift, the savings isn't worth the aggravation.

I know some people who wouldn't give up. My mother, for instance, is an avid coupon user (see above). There are some thirty or forty possible promo codes, why not try each one. They might say it's the principle of the thing. They might say you don't get rich by spending more money than you have to. They might say the meal will taste better having gotten the code. That's their choice. I am already hungry. I want to enjoy my goat, my rice, my mango chutney. I know, by now, it will taste exactly the same whatever I spend on it. It will not taste the same if I am aggravated. Worse, I know if I wait too long, I will be overly hungry, eat too quickly, and forget the pleasure of taste.

IN ALL THIS, I AM REMINDED THAT I LIVE IN ABUNDANCE. IT'S ABOUT TWO DEGREES outside, not including wind chill, and the temperature continues its steady decline. Snow falls in small hard particles, blowing in spirals like dust motes in a stream of sunlight. The delivery person who has to come out in weather like tonight's probably does not have the option for take-out.

How fortunate I felt as a child when my mother could afford to order in a pizza or we could eat out. I remember, too, one time, when we were perhaps at our poorest, when she left for a day to go Christmas shopping, and said she would bring home Chinese food. The three of us kids were so excited, that we set the table with plates and bowls, flatware and cups for tea. During her long day out, she had parked in a no parking area, and her car ad been towed. The dinner money went to get the car out of the tow lot, so all she could afford was wonton soup. It wasn't the first soup-only meal for us, but it was the most disappointing.

OUR SOCIAL MEDIA FEEDS, THE VARIOUS ADVERTISEMENTS WE SEE WHEREVER we look, the new car the neighbor gets all can make us keenly aware of what we don't have. The fact is I live in abundance. The fact is I have to remind myself of this. The fact is there is much I'd like but don't have. The fact is I make decisions everyday about what I can afford and what I can't. This makes me not unlike so many others in this country, in this world. Twice I've gone into credit counseling. I work two jobs sometimes, and hustle at others to make money in other ways.

Still, I give money to 80 percent of the homeless and panhandlers who approach me. I support various organizations and charities. I donate regularly to a literary arts organization to bring writers out. I promote punk shows in my home community, often guaranteeing bands with money out-of-pocket to insure they come play where I live. I like to see my community come out. Each of these concerts and readings is a celebration. The bands and writers often stay at my house.

What I've discovered is that inclusiveness not exclusiveness has brought more joy to me more than anything I might buy. Even this emphasizes my privilege and good fortune.

AND STILL HAPPINESS, LIKE A GASEOUS MONSTER IN A CLASSIC Star Trek episode, maintains its elusiveness. Perhaps that's why we're given the right to pursue it as long as it doesn't hurt others. Like all pursuits, part of the joy should be in the activity. Many of the hunters I know—whether they hunt duck, deer, morel mushrooms, or the perfect landscape to photograph—tell me that there's a thrill in the hunt that has nothing to do with the result. That's something Elmer Fudd never understood. My friend Dan would go out with the start of bow season to hunt whitetails. He'd leave early in the morning, just as dawn opened its eyelids, dressed in camo, and drive out to his secret spots. He loved the smell of the woods, particularly the mornings after a good rain, and he could talk for fifteen minutes just about the morning sounds in the trees. More days than not, he never saw a deer, and sometimes he did, but didn't bag it. Those days weren't bad days. Those days were the joy.

Some people might blanch at this, ask how killing deer could be a joy. We get caught up in how others find their happiness: I could give all the arguments for why deer hunting is a good thing from deer population maintenance to my own enjoyment of venison, but this isn't that sort of book. Rather, this emphasizes how we get caught up in judging how other people find their happiness rather than focusing on our own choices to find ours. For some it's in the yoga studio, the weight room, the kitchen, the church or the woods. Find your bliss, the self-help books say.

Judge not lest you be judged, Jesus says.

What is so amazing about judging people for what they do to make themselves happy is how much time and attention it takes from our own sense of happiness. How much angst it causes. It distracts us from our own path, to see someone on theirs.

Consumer capitalism offers a solution: instant gratification. Buy something to distract yourself. Yes, it'll give you a momentary rush of success, but when that fades you need to take out your credit card again, buy something else. Shopping can become an addiction, the search for that rush. I've known some die-hard shoppers, listened to them discuss the perfect find. And how a week later they're out shopping again.

PERHAPS I CAN BLAME ARISTOTLE, WHOM I LIKE SO MUCH THAT I ALMOST NAMED a cat after him. The Greek philosopher believed happiness stems from achieving, over one's lifetime, all the goods—health, wealth, knowledge, friends, yadda yadda yadda—that lead to the perfection of human nature and enrich a life. Like the Pokémon cards my son used to play with, "gotta catch them all."

Or perhaps Aristotle was more nuanced than that, he also believed that Good was a mean between two extremes: could one have too much wealth? Too many friends that one can't do right by all of them? Can one have too much knowledge that they began to suffer with what they know? We have to be aware of what is Good for us. We have to discover that mean between two extremes and live within out means, so to speak.

So perhaps Aristotle was building on Socrates's teaching about happiness; Socrates rejected the idea that happiness derived from physical or external conditions, such as pleasure or wealth. Rather, Socrates that happiness might be found in living a life that's right for one's soul, a life that satisfied one's greater good. Often, though, that's hard to do, when one is challenged by others' expectations.

ARLIER I SAID THAT IN CHILDHOOD WE FORM *OUR BELIEFS IN WHAT WILL make us happy.* It's this language, now, I wish I'd never learned. In consumerist cultures people constantly look for what they can get that will bring them momentary pleasure, and we call it "happiness," as if happiness can be delivered, as if it can be gift wrapped. Thanks Amazon! It was John Stuart Mill who discussed the differences of pleasure. How often did I think an object, a capacity, a person, a publication would change my fortune and make me happy? Worse, I've lived by a similar philosophy in my love life, thinking one lover or another, one partner or another, could bring with them happiness. Of course not. Those relationship failed, often with a lot of pain to the other person and to myself. These things both add to my shame and are connected to it. How funny misery is self-perpetuating. My hurting of others surely shows how misery loves company.

The fact is I often tried to protect those I loved—truly cared deeply about and valued their joy—from the very hurtful things I was doing. Sometimes a lie is designed to protect the self. Sometimes, a lie is to protect the person we're lying to. Sometimes both. Non-duality. I learned to lie from my mother. I learned to lie from my father. I learned to lie to protect the hurt and scared self, to hide from my own unhappiness.

A scene that repeats from my childhood: riding in the car with my mother, she says once we reach our destination, I will be happy. I am confused because I am not in those moments unhappy. Antsy, perhaps. Bummed or frustrated because instead of doing something else I'd rather be doing. I'm going to be out with my mother. But I'm not unhappy. No destination could make me happier though some might lessen my frustration. Being in the passenger seat beside her, she who'd been at work so much, is the happiness.

Sometimes people ask me about my Buddhist beliefs and American culture because the values of consumer capitalism and the values of Buddhism seem at odds. (I might argue, but don't, that Christian beliefs and American culture also seem at odds.) After all the second noble truth is "All desiring leads to suffering," and I have ambition for my work, for my students, for my friends, for my son. These people say it snarkily: "If you're so zen," (yes, I've been asked this question in just these words), "why do you care so much about your career?" (Feel free to erase "career" and fill in the blank with *MGB* or *record collection* or *what publisher takes your next book*.)

There is a difference between aspiring and desiring. There is a difference between attachment, unattachment, and detachment. My aspirations are part of my happiness and a reminder of the suffering of desire. My ownership of things doesn't mean I don't recognize that I don't need them. If I didn't have them, if I suddenly had to sell the MG for some reason, I wouldn't be unhappy. It might cause me grief. I surely would miss it. I might be upset that I had to sell it for whatever reason, but the joy driving with the top down provides is just that, a momentary joy.

JOY IS NOT HAPPINESS. JOY IS MOMENTARY. DITTO SADNESS. I LIVE fully in my moments of joy. That's why I laugh, why I sing some song I love when I hear it, even in the supermarket. Buddhism focuses on the fleeting nature of experience, of how we experience things. Playing music, driving, talking to friends, playing a video game with my son, writing: all these bring gladness to me in moments. I try to make sure there are more of these moments than moments that bring me sadness. I write this alone in my room in Pittsburgh on what it the coldest night of the year, and I'm glad: glad for the task, glad for the warmth of the room, glad for the work that has brought me. And I do have work to do.

That's part of being happy.

IF SADNESS IS THE OPPOSITE OF JOY, WHAT MIGHT BE THE OPPOSITE OF HAPPINESS? I've spent time thinking about this. I used to think it was "depression," but I've come to understand this is a clinical term. Sadness, perhaps is a possible antonym; however, the more I think about it, now, I claim that the antithesis of happiness is anger.

Like happiness, anger is a force for action. My old high school guidance counselor, Wendy Sands, used to suggest the sublimated anger led to sadness. Maybe it does. Consider how good one feels after expressing their anger. This is the philosophy behind primal scream therapy: to release anger is to often be happier.

Being frustrated to find joy makes me angry. Expressing, freely, my anger releases it and opens up the possibility for joy. Sadness offers no release; it is a limbo state.

I STARTED WRITING POETRY SERIOUSLY AS A TEENAGER, WEARING BLACK, LISTENING to punk and goth bands, going to shows, while feeling excluded from mainstream society. I chose this exclusion, the principal at my first high school suggested, and maybe he was right, but so many factors of biography, particularly my shame and sublimated anger, prevented me from feeling welcome by such society. I wrote poems about my alienation. I wrote poems about my insecurities, my secret crushes, my heartaches in black marble notebooks I would buy for 25 cents each, filling them up with Bic ball point ink. These were attempts at self-expression: I hadn't learned anything about actually *writing* poems, and that's okay. These scribbles led to my study of poetry, but at 16, 17, 18 I was just trying to give voice to what couldn't be said at the dinner table, at morning coffee, from the passenger seat of my mother's car.

My mother would read some of these, and once she asked me why so many of my poems were so sad. Having spoken to young writers for years (and sometimes their parents) I know that this experience isn't isolated. *Why do you always write about sad things?*

The fact is as a teenager I wrote about sad things because when I felt bad, I needed to do something with my sadness: it prevented me from doing anything else. When I felt elation, I was too busy doing what was giving me joy to stop and write poems about it. Rock n roll. Skateboarding. Those late-night talks about art with bad diner coffee. Riding the subway to Coney Island just to laugh along the boardwalk with friends, tossing leftover hotdog bun to the seagulls. Whatever I was doing with all that enthusiasm and excitement, I was *doing* it. It seems kind of obvious: like so many of us in our joy, I was living in the moment.

CONEY ISLAND. I LOOKED FORWARD TO SEEING THE SKELETAL FRAME of the old parachute drop first, then the arc of the Wonder Wheel, then the hills of the Cyclone appear as the train approached, building our anticipation. We'd break out of the train and rush toward the street, the boardwalk, the beach side arcade, Nathan's.

Coney Island existed, always, as a place of escape, particularly for us who saw ourselves as part Warrior and part Freak Show freak with our dyed hair and tattoos, with my mohawk and freedom.

Coney Island. Still today, I make a pilgrimage there every summer. Only a few weeks ago I got a copy of a sketch my then-girlfriend did of my punk uniform: those combat boots, ripped jeans, my kilt of a flannel shirt, arms tied at my waist. Like so many of my teenage friends, she was driven by art, by not wanting to do what was expected of her by our families, by 1980s television. Like so many of us, she succeeded, founding her own fashion company. More, though, she became a person unmoored from what people think of her. She tells me it's key to her well-being.

We didn't dress for the beach: those spikes at my wrist, those studs on a denim vest, those band t-shirts—The Damned, The Misfits, Dead Kennedys, Black Flag, The Germs—were all there to keep people away. The stories we told were familiar, each highlighting a history that might include schizophrenic mothers, abuse, bullying. We were outcasts because we'd been cast out: a brigade of Adams and Eves. The leather jacket I'd put on come colder weather became a metaphor. What's a biker jacket designed to do but protect the motorcyclist from road rash? The road I'd known had bruised me, battered me. I unzipped that jacket for Laura, sure; unzipped it for my friends. But more often than not that jacket kept me protected, kept threatening people away, the way I hoped my eyes could.

And always my canvas bag, whatever book I was reading, the marble notebook, the black pens.

THE FACT IS I LOVE THE PROCESS OF WRITING: POEMS, STORIES, NOVELS, SONGS, even this treatise on happiness: I love the search for the right word, the accurate phrasing. Part of it is the exploratory nature of writing. I never work with an outline, never know in advance what will come out. Think Alice in Wonderland: "How do I know what I think until I see what I say?" I don't know where a poem is going to take me. I'm out in the woods looking for mushrooms. Sometimes I get to the end of two hours of pen on paper, and I have a draft of something I will want to continue working on. Sometimes I have some lines that maybe will lead me to a poem. Sometimes I end up with a number of wadded up balls of paper. Sometimes morels grow in abundance. Sometimes not. They may be on the south side of the highway and you're in the woods on the north side. Yet you come out of the woods, flushed with exercise, spring warmth deep in your lungs. That, in and of itself, is a victory.

Not today, when the snow makes apparitions outside. Mushroom season is still several months away, and Buddhism teaches to live in the now, to be mindful, to not spend too much time looking beyond this moment, which is beautiful and which is ours. Therefore, I look at these words again, wonder what I'm doing. Trust it'll come to me if I keep paying attention.

I HAVE NEVER SAID I WAS A GOOD BUDDHIST, THOUGH PERHAPS I AM A BETTER Buddhist than I was Roman Catholic. Truth be told, I have no attachment to being labeled a good Buddhist. I don't sit lotus as my knees hurt too much when I try, and I rarely meditate for more than fifteen minutes. Despite the reveries I keep for the past in my work, and even in this essay, I keep in mind that those days, that Gerard LaFemina, doesn't exist anymore. They were just part of the process of becoming now's Gerry LaFemina. Tomorrow's Gerry LaFemina doesn't exist yet and any number of things could happen between now and then that would prevent him from being, that would summon forth a somewhat different Gerry LaFemina.

Identity, this thing we carry with us, both how others see us and how we see ourselves, based on not what is remembered of experience, but what is remembered about remembering,

Catholicism taught me St. Peter kept a ledger and beside my name (perhaps the 21st century St. Peter is running a spreadsheet on a tablet now to make things easier) he had a tally. Everything I had done, good and bad, kept on this list, and it would be tallied up, like a credit card account (how many purchases did I indulge in, how many payments did I make). That's a lot of shame. I could confess my sins, but I had to make sure that I confessed them all. Only then could I be forgiven.

None of the nuns at St. Charles talked about happiness, though they focused on sin and pleasure and the evils of spoiling yourself. They understood shame. They talked about the seven deadly sins, the cardinal sins. We were tested to make sure we knew their names. The minor were venal, but still sins. We were kids in tartan plaid and dark green uniforms, most of us from families reaching for the bottom rung of middle classness; others higher up. Our heroes were actors, musicians, athletes because our parents wanted us to have better lives than they had, and because they seemed to have achieved the "American Dream." We lived on streets, in houses where for some of us, I know now, cruelties happened. Many of our parents drank or gambled or fucked their way to divorces. Domestic violence was potentially rampant. I knew only the public lives of my classmates, just as I only saw the nuns in their habits and wimples. Years later, shopping with my mother, I ran into my old principal, Sister Jeanine, and she was in street clothes. She was no one I knew.

I had been molested and most people didn't know for the very same reason. Cruelties were perpetuated, no doubt, on every street. Still, people insisted we lived in a good neighborhood. So much sinning, no wonder we were taught the Act of Contrition. No one focused on the virtues. What did we know about Chastity, Temperance, Charity, Diligence, Patience, Kindness, and Humility.

THERE ARE NO VIRTUES WITHOUT THE SEVEN DEADLY SINS: GLUTTONY, lust, avarice, pride, despair, vainglory, and sloth. No positive charge without a negative charge. Non-duality. Every battery demonstrates this. Every physicist understands. Who hasn't indulged in some of these? Worse, who hasn't in virtuousness suffered pride and vainglory? Irony isn't lost in the search for happiness.

We live in a time of irony, a time when being cool and detached is a stance that leads to less hurt and less reward. If our actions are ironic, then nothing is at stake. Happiness requires living with something at stake. In this it's unlike the cool of Fonzie, who loved his adopted family and his friends. Kierkegaard declared, "Life is not a problem to be solved but a reality to be experienced." Irony mediates our ability to experience things in their full spectrum. Ask the motorcyclists who want to ride without helmets: they accept it's a risk, but the risk comes with rewards those of us in cars can't understand.

Nearly 20 years ago, I went to see Tom Jones perform at a casino in Michigan. I went because I thought it would be a gag. I went, dare I say it, as a practice in irony. In my mind, then, Jones was "cheesy" and his playing in a casino in what might be described as the middle of nowhere in the Midwest seemed like a set up. I was living in a small Michigan town at the time and had little to do most nights, so I saw this as a way to get some kicks. The audience would be a hoot, I told myself: the songs would be straight out of my mother's record collection from right before I was born, and I could sit in the back and take notes. Such was my arrogance.

In fact: Jones blew me away. He was Tom Jones, after all. He threw the microphone from left hand to right. He danced in his manly fashion that he mastered in the 1960s. He was gracious, grateful to be performing, and generous with his set, playing nearly two hours. He put on a show. He loved his songs, loved singing them, loved his band, loved his audience. There's really no other way to say it: he blew me away. I sang along with "What's New Pussycat?" and "It's Not Unusual" and laughed, not with smugness but a kind of glee that was surprising, when women still threw bras and panties at him on stage. At set's end I was glad for the encores, and clapped until my hands stung. It would have been terrible to have maintained the filter of irony for I would have lost so much.

Happiness is not unusual.

I KNOW LITTLE OF TOM JONES'S BIOGRAPHY. I'D IMAGINE, LIKE MANY CELEBRITIES, he has suffered in ways I can barely imagine. He has also had numerous joys. What I appreciated about that performance was how he gave it his all. He loved his audience: be it at the Royal Albert Hall or the Turtle Creek Casino. He was a performer; he was there to perform.

As the Zen saying puts it, "Before enlightenment, chop wood and carry water. After enlightenment, chop wood and carry water." Work is what we do. For better or worse it defines us; not just what we do, but how we choose to do it.

Work is work. Our lives don't change with fame or a degree or enlightenment. The abundance we live in comes with responsibilities. The professional athlete trains as hard as those trying to make it to the big show. For many, that work is a calling. To watch someone great practice that thing which they love is to watch someone work, yes, but also to watch someone be thoroughly involved in their dedication, their talent, their self. We might call this a vocation.

Once I heard an interview with Tony Bennett on NPR's *Fresh Air*. He discussed the struggles of addicts, including Amy Winehouse and his own battles. If I remember correctly, it was his manager that said to him "Never sin against your talent." It helped turn his life around. Think about the baseball greats tainted by steroid and the P.E.D. era: how they didn't have faith in their talent alone and how they sinned against it. I love that statement. Never sin against your talent is surely one of my guides to happiness.

SOME READERS MIGHT BE WONDERING ABOUT MY GOING ON ABOUT TOM JONES and Tony Bennett. It's not very punk rock. It's not very "cool." I'm interested in being a good punk rocker in the same way I'm interested in being a good Buddhist, which is to say, very little.

Too much of my life I've spent working hard to be cool, wearing a kind of ironic detachment, and worrying more about how people perceived me rather than who I am. This has led to various types of duplicities on my part, none of which I am proud of. We learn our masks early on: my mother worked hard to maintain a level of middle-class appearances. I was taught not to cry because it was unmanly. I hid my molestation for years, and I know people who hid their sexual preferences, their abusive boyfriends and spouses, their struggles with depression and anxiety for too long, often leading to drug use or alcoholism or nihilism. Think Amy Winehouse. Think Kurt Cobain. Think Anthony Bourdain.

We learn to wear masks early. I became a writer to express myself about things I couldn't otherwise say. I became a punk to outwardly express the turmoil and anger and hurt I felt. But there was writer mask and punk mask—more a black leather jacket to keep me protected—, and later a mask of a spouse, father, professor, editor … Often I protected the masks, what people perceived of me in different situations, more than I took care of the me behind the masks. At a certain point, I even lost sight of who that me was.

We learn our masks early. What would my classmates think? The nuns? The priests? My mom?

So much of my life was spent insecure about my status, about what other's thought. Giving that up was not an act of privilege but an act of courage, and in doing so I became available to happiness.

I N *Bridge on the River Kwai,* Colonel Saito says "Be happy in your work." Hard to do sometimes, particularly as prisoners of war in a work camp. Hard to do coming home smelling like French fry grease or exhausted from a day in the heat hammering shingles into place, sweat and callouses all. I've come home like that. I'd watched my mother work. I'd watched my great aunt, who still cleaned offices in her seventies, and for whom my mother would sometimes substitute, emptying garbage cans and wiping down desks after a long day at the office. Work was work. People did it, and they did it as best they could.

They did it even when they didn't love it because for many, work provided the capacity to afford the things they loved doing. My mother defined her vocation for years as doing right by her three kids, opening up opportunity, even when it took three jobs, even when it was hard. We've lost sight of that as a culture: that sense of responsibility and pride in the work. The men who worked the mills and mines, the women who worked the offices and classrooms back in a time of more traditional gender roles had a mission: provide. These days, when jobs don't seem to provide enough for a family to live because the jobs and their pay are equally nominal; more, when any body seems replaceable, when the job is unstimulating and can be done by anybody, that sense of vocation feels ripped from us.

I knew a hockey coach who used to say the value of the name on the front of their jerseys was only equal to the value each player put on the name on the back of each one. If only corporate America felt that way: if only we valued workers and their work, we might see some rise in community happiness.

Time and again I tell my students what they hand in to me reflects how they want me to perceive them. I am not talking about right and wrong answers, mind you, but by the quality of the workmanship. How well do we strive to be our best?

My first teaching job was at Kirtland Community College in Roscommon,

Michigan. It was a school of some 1300 students, serving four counties of mostly state and federal lands; the majority of the students came from families that supplemented their paychecks with fishing and hunting provided meals, and they came from underfunded school districts. The nearest town was St. Helen, and some people in the community referred to the school as the St. Helen Institute for Technology.

Once I heard a student say about an assignment "It's good enough for Kirtland," and I inquired what that meant. He explained that "It didn't really matter how much work he put into it. It was just *Kirtland*."

Good enough is not good.

We train ourselves in terms of our expectations of ourselves. If we keep thinking good enough is good, we start thinking that we aren't worthy of goodness, of happiness. We settle.

FOUL! HOW CAN WE BE GRATEFUL FOR WHAT WE HAVE AND NOT SETTLE?

This is where I make the distinction between aspiring and desiring. Desiring focuses on end results: *I desire this publication, this item, this person.* I am not talking about end results. I am talking about aspiring, and by that, I mean process. I don't know what the publication result of this project will be, for instance, but I aspire to write the best book on "happiness" that I can. I don't know what the end result of my next relationship will be, but I aspire to be the best lover/partner I can be. I have often failed as a parent, as a poet, as a performer, but never failed to give it my all even if it didn't measure up, even if I was limited by my own shortcomings. Aspiration is about what's in my control, the means by which I do things, the means by which I live.

The abundance is in me.

Desire is about outcomes. I can't control whether an editor will want to publish this book, whether my next girlfriend will want to stay in a relationship with me long term. That hockey coach knew that he and his players couldn't control the outcome of every game, but they could control how they played each shift, each period. What's important is that we take care of what's in our control.

Buddhism teaches that desire equals suffering. I can't argue with that. Aspiring leads to satisfaction whatever the outcome.

EVEN THIS IS ALL WRITTEN FROM A POINT OF PRIVILEGE. FOR MANY, CAPITALISM didn't afford even that; and now it's worse. Service industry jobs provide little security, often pay low wages, and thus require workers to take on second jobs or side hustles to make sure the bills are paid. There's little time for many to dedicate to a vocation. I went to graduate school with people who now teach multiple adjunct classes at three or four different institutions and no longer have time and energy to dedicate to writing fiction or poems like they love to do and that they aspire to do well.

The so-called gig economy that creates independent contractors of so many may sometimes pay a decent enough wage to provide a better safety net, but it also often undoes that safety net by removing benefits packages and requiring workers to handle their own income tax liability. Such "self-employment" further alienates workers from the community and culture of a given organization, removing them from the shared goals and team work that can provide a sense of purpose and belonging.

This sense of purpose and belonging has to do with the social aspects of the workplace and the way the work is perceived by the greater society. To look down upon the work of someone, say the supermarket cashier who has recently wished you a happy holiday, is to deprive them the dignity of their work, to isolate them from some approved cultural norm. I see this sometimes: someone will talk on their cell phone while a checkout worker scans canned goods, thus suggesting the worker isn't worth their engagement, is somehow less than them. We ignore the dignity of their work.

The best workplaces work against this by valuing workers and their work: whether it be through holiday parties and bonuses, workplace March Madness brackets, a workplace softball team, benefits designed to make workers valued (consider, Henry Ford wanted his workers to earn enough that they could buy Ford Model Ts, creating a shared sense of pride in the vehicle), or worker stock options, corporate culture can do a lot for both workplace morale and worker morale. When I see my friends who adjunct, who work the gig economy, or who work low-paying service economy jobs, I see people excluded from the opportunity to feel part of a workplace cultural community, and thus removed from one source of satisfaction in one's labor.

I N THE SUMMARY OF ITS FINDINGS, THE WORLD HAPPINESS REPORT NOTES that "Unemployment causes a major fall in happiness, and even for those in work the quality of work can cause major variations in happiness." This isn't a surprise: adult full-time workers spend at least eight hours a day at work, which means one-third (at least) of most days is spent working. Add to it transportation time, training sessions, and what have you, it can be more of that. Work, therefore, is a significant player in how we see ourselves, our value, our relationship with others.

When I sit on an airplane and I am asked by a fellow passenger what I do, if I say "professor" I get a very different reaction than if I say "poet." A professor has mainstream "value" in a way that "poet" does not. (For the record, I only said "poet" as part of an experiment. When it comes to my career, I'm a professor, and one of the things I teach is poetry. That said, both writing poetry and teaching feel like vocations to me: they are parallel tracks.) Some of the value that comes from work is its "role" in society, although sometimes that role isn't always compensated financially in the same manner as it is esteemed: most people love teachers and can still name their favorites from years ago, but they don't want to raise their taxes to pay teachers more.

Still, vocations remain a luxury for many. In general, the economic security of white-collar jobs provides a greater sense of happiness in those workers than experienced by blue-collar workers, whose work is not only more often less secure but also physically more intense. Bodies in physical discomfort are more likely to be unhappy, as physical stress is a type of insecurity. Despite this, I know so many miserable people of wealth and means. No doubt the fear of losing what they have fills them with dread. For many, the more they have to lose, the greater their insecurity, so much so a whole industry of 'fear capitalism' has risen with commercials of staged break-ins designed to exploit that insecurity.

Think of Elmer Fudd, his face burnt and blackened from a shotgun mishap: that's the physical manifestation of his unhappiness.

MUCH OF THIS HAS TO DO WITH HAVING A SENSE OF PURPOSE. Goals, studies show, are a part of a happy life. Goal-oriented individuals usually have a more positive approach and outlook towards life. But goals can also create an unhealthy set of desires. Goal setting, done right, can help us perceive failures as temporary setbacks, rather than personal shortcomings.

Do what makes you happy, the cliché goes. This is what an uncle or aunt or guidance counselor says at a high school graduation.

Do what makes you happy. YOLO. Friends say.

Unfortunately, people think this means "do what gives you pleasure," and that's how things fall apart: pleasure is not happiness. As a matter of fact, much of the work I do to contribute to my own happiness is hard and often unpleasurable. When I'm on my back on a concrete floor, and it's 90 degrees in the garage and I'm aware that three inches above my head is 1800 pounds of steel being held up by jack stands, sweat stinging my eyes, a wrench in my greasy right hand, pleasure isn't particularly what I'm experiencing. Then the wrench slips, my hand bangs against the underbody of the car, and the whole chassis shakes for a moment of "oh shit." I feel the skin tear, blood joins the grease and sweat. It may get infected. It wouldn't be the first time that happened. Fortunately, my tetanus shot is up to date.

I'll wriggle myself out from under the MG. I'll curse. Clean up and bandage my hand as best as possible. Then I'll get back on the concrete floor, push myself back under the car. A few minutes later the bandage has slipped out of place.

This isn't fun. This is work. It affords me the later pleasure of driving the car with the top down. There's a clear purpose to this work. And also, great satisfaction when the job is finished and the car runs again, runs better, problem solved. No one solved it for me, though I have a community of fellow enthusiasts I can reach out to for advice when I'm stuck.

The goal is that I will do what it takes to get the car running. That satisfaction might be a route to happiness. It's similar to how I feel when I finish cooking a complicated dinner idea that I'd never tried before and my family enjoys it. It's similar to how I feel when I see a student overcome a problem with the help of my guidance. It's similar to how I feel when a poem comes together after months of drafting it. These are deep satisfactions centered in accomplishment.

Pleasure offers satisfaction with little effort, often it comes in the form of distraction of the work that needs to be done. Sure, I might be able to pay to have a local mechanic fix the MG, but it doesn't provide the sense of satisfaction that wrenching does.

In other words, often what gives us pleasure, actually delays our happiness.

I TAKE A BREAK, WALK THE THREE ROOMS OF MY GUEST SUITE, CONSIDER a small piece of chocolate that will stimulate the palate, perhaps calm my hunger. How much I enjoy the rush of sugar, the smoothness of milk chocolate, that texture as I bite into it, feel it melt slightly on my tongue. The sensual pleasures are hard to ignore.

The duck watches me whenever I enter the room. I'm ridiculous.

I think about picking up the guitar, strum some chords. It's a way of distracting myself from my hunger, and a way of distracting myself from this work, this thinking about happiness, which isn't particularly pleasurable. Already I hear my friends arguing with me, disappointed in me, seeing me as failing the working class.

Instead, I sit back down, open up my social media account, begin to read what others have posted, see that a few people have liked and responded to my last post. A little rush of adrenaline and endorphins runs through my body, and I click to see what's happened. A minute later, as I still scroll through my timeline, I realize I've not written anything of this treatise on happiness in several minutes. I think to call the restaurant, but the driver is out, and there's nothing that can be done other than take some pleasure in my complaining. So many people enjoy the sound of their own voice, their self-righteousness.

I close the internet browser, return to the blank page. I don't know what to write, and that's frustrating. I'm embarrassed at myself for going to Facebook, for giving into the temptation of its pleasures: the smiling faces of friends far away, the acknowledgment of warmer weather elsewhere, the good news in the worlds of publishing and love and family. All of it distraction, all of it a guilty pleasure.

I USED TO PLAY BASKETBALL WITH MY DEAN AT KIRTLAND: A CHICAGOAN, former Psychology professor old enough to be my dad. Our basketball games were competitive, though I admit to lacking a particular "killer instinct" in sports. Winning doesn't matter to me as I don't equate winning with any particular success. It will not make me happy just as losing will not make me unhappy (though I will admit to having been frustrated by any number of losses in my life as an athlete: such responses were not about "losing" but about my performance, about letting myself and my teammates down). What matters to me is the process of the game, which includes the social interaction, the living in the village of the ball court.

We'd play in the afternoon in the community center in Roscommon, Michigan. We'd talk food and women and sports. We were guys in the United States in the mid-1990s. He was one in a sequence of men who were father figures in my life, someone I'm grateful for.

We'd play in the later afternoon. Running lay ups, dodging fouls, stopping suddenly to pop a jump shot toward the rim. Hitting it, the defender would now get the ball at half court, check the rock. And there was chatter. Always chatter.

We'd play. Play is such an interesting word: it's a word that means to have leisure time, to enjoy one's self. Even when it's work, it's play. I know many people who put more effort into their play than they do into their work. When I write, I remind myself I'm playing with language: the elasticity and plasticity of it, exploring its potential to make something new.

It wasn't easy to live in Roscommon and later Grayling. I was single, from New York, yet in a town of 1100 people, most of them well under the poverty line, under educated, under employed, and under the radar of the state and federal governments. I would often drive an hour away with a cooler in the car so I could get better groceries. Dating was hard to do. Finding people with similar interests even as friends proved difficult. Yet as a dean, Rich worked hard to let me run readings and bring poetry to the area. He supported the possibility of culture as a resource not for me but for the community at large. It could be, he realized, a doorway for community members out of their environment, if only briefly.

Often, I felt my own malaise, a bitterness of living in a state of aloneness that rubbed against my personality and history. In this way I was like many of my neighbors who felt isolated from mainstream culture or had abandoned cities and suburbs down state to self-isolate. I chose my own isolation even as I had a community of good people around me who made it clear I was welcome. Still, I declared to myself, I was unhappy.

Rich stared at me, ball under his left arm against his flank. "Why do you think you have the right to be happy?"

I stammered without an answer. And I lost the game.

How often have I lived like this?

If only I could date _____, I'd be happy.
If only I had _____, I'd be happy.
If only I had _____, I'd be happier.
If only I had _____, I'd be really fucking happy.

Doesn't matter how many times I filled in one of those blanks, none of it brought me happiness. It may have satisfied a want, but wants are like planes waiting to land at the airport. One gets on the ground, and another is waiting for the runway to open.

That's not to say dating _____ or having _____ didn't provide pleasures. Though, more often than not, what I found attractive about the person I wanted to date was connected to less attractive attributes that I hadn't seen because we weren't dating. They weren't part of their public selves. Nonduality.

Having an MG is great fun when I'm driving the mountain roads of western Maryland. It's less fun, when the car is on jack stands, and I'm sliding under it on my back, the transmissions and oil pan only inches from my head. I've been under the car trying to figure out what's wrong with the speedometer angle drive, or is it the parking brake assembly, or is it just a routine oil change. The cement floor of the garage doesn't get more comfortable over time. Or the car has broken down somewhere, because the alternator stopped charging the battery, most likely because of something I forgot to reconnect. Suddenly, I'm angry, frustrated, and pained. All of these things are natural reactions.

I'm not a mechanic, though when I taught at Kirtland Community College, when I bought the MG, the school had an automotive lab, and there I learned a few things by automotive teachers. Then I have a network of friends who are MG folks who help me troubleshoot, who talk me down so I can re-envision the situation. This community makes me feel included, reassures me that problems can be solved. It's good to walk away, do something else. The only thing I lose in those moments are a few hours, another day of driving, whatever. What I regain is perspective, insight, focus.

It's good to remind myself of certain truths: if I want to drive the car, if I want to feel safe in it, I better do this job right. The pleasure comes with some work. Because I'm no mechanic, it may take a while: tomorrow or the next day or someday next week, I'll be driving, top down, enjoying the moment thoroughly. Pursuing happiness.

Let's not forget: it's January. I'm a two-hour drive from home where the MG sits in the garage. Out the window the temperature has dropped some more and all I can see is snow pinwheeling.

THINGS DON'T BRING HAPPINESS. THINGS ARE EXTERNAL. Things are outside the self. Another person, ditto. Our sports team winning, ditto. A better job, ditto. Some praise for work well done, ditto. Even this dinner I wait for can't bring happiness, though it can do away with the petty pangs of hunger, the discomfort of wanting to eat. What is outside of us is just that, outside of us: we might subsume it or consume it, but it is not us.

Happiness is some aspect of us: friends I've known who have come out of the closet, even at the expense of familial relationships have said they are much happier now, despite the sadness they feel being estranged from their family, because they are finally living to satisfy their personal sense of who they are. They external approval of mom and dad may have avoided conflict but it did little to make themselves happy.

How often have I failed because I was worrying about disappointing someone in my life? How often have I failed because I resented those others and resented myself for giving in to my fears and thus sabotaged myself? How often have I worried about image? Cowardice and shame are linked. I cheated on my ex-wife because I was unhappy, because I blamed her for my unhappiness when it came from within; but also, because I was too scared of looking like a failure to end my marriage first. I was too scared of letting people down, including her.

A contradiction? Surely, but one that is echoed by the experience of many. Conversations among the many I know who have done similar things, men and women, straight and gay alike, emphasize that this way of thinking is not uncommon. By giving up the belief my partner should make me happy, I've returned the power of my happiness to myself, and I can allow for my relationship to be a source of joy, pleasure, aggravation, frustration, disappointment, and surprise without it ever being unhappy.

SHAME IS AN OLD FRIEND. AFTER I FIRST ACKNOWLEDGED BEING MOLESTED, I thought I was free of shame. The fact is I learned to replace one shameful secret with another. I filled the hole without ever making myself whole. In addiction recovery circle they would call something similar being a dry drunk. I dealt with the problem but didn't deal with the causes of the problem. Cheating on my wife was just another way to welcome my old pal shame back in my life. I knew who I was when carrying shame with me. Without it, I longed for the comfort of a shameful secret, even though such a secret caused me discomfort.

Which means I didn't know who I was.

The space where I kept the shame asked to be filled. What filled it best? A new shame. It's almost as if I were addicted to my sense of shame, my sense of secrets, my sense of surviving what I knew I could survive.

I come from a family that doesn't talk much. Having secrets is what we knew. Even now, writing about some of these things, I feel a discomfort about revealing too much. After all, my poems stray far from the autobiographical, and rooted in some other me that shares some perceptions about the world. This though, to talk about my shame, is both scary and affirming. I didn't suspect to write about it, but here it is, so natural, it seems like I knew I would all along. The path is the path.

So often we give up the driver's seat of our happiness, look for it to come as if by UPS or the post man, but know. It is ours. We have to learn to drive it.

IN THE PASSENGER SEAT OF MY MOTHER'S CAR, THAT BROWN PLYMOUTH DUSTER of the early seventies, I'd sing along with the radio songs. AM hits like the Turtles, who promised we'd be happy together. Blood, Sweat, & Tears declaring, "You've made me so, very happy…"

Is it any wonder we think happiness is something given to us by others as opposed to being something we have a priori. Someone makes us "Happy together." And with those songs comes the fantasy of eternal love without strife or heartache or difficulty. It's the pop song equivalent of happily ever after.

If only I had looked at the lyrics of "Help" more closely, I might have learned something. I was a Beatles fan as a young child (and once got gonged in a *Gong Show*-style talent contest at the age of six lip-synching "I Wanna Hold Your Hand"). Paul and John understood the relationship of happiness to insecurity, the call for help going out only when "every now and then I feel so insecure, I know that I just need you like I've never done before."

The relationship in "Help" is undefined, more complicated, and more understanding of the need for a community of friends to reenforce that sense of security.

SOME MIGHT BE SURPRISED BY MY EARLY LOVE OF THE BEATLES. But as a kid I loved them. I remember listening to their records in a friend's basement after school: it was his parent's cabinet stereo with the long spindle that allowed us to stack records so that the next platter would fall when the side of the record playing finished. I remember the joy I felt, seeing *Beatlemania* with my aunt Irene at the Wintergarden Theater on Broadway. I am not ashamed singing along with even the sappiest of the Beatles oeuvre.

Guilty pleasures: pleasures that our mask won't let us admit, such things that we are embarrassed of because they give us joy. Why should anything that gives us joy embarrass us? The hedonist in me suggests as long as it hurts no one and nothing, why should it matter that I sing along with Tom Jones's "It's not Unusual'? The vainglorious in me worries about what my cool friends would think.

I find a video of Tom Jones singing, crank up the volume, and let it rip, the way I would with the top down so I can hear the music above the wind.

Punk provided that community for me. The bands I played in, the friends I made on the scene all emphasized an us vs them sensibility. Some people continue to consider punk as being nihilistic, wanting to smash the state, and yes, that's a part of punk rock: the state, for many, was the source of their insecurity; more, in a socio-historical context, the late 1970s that birthed the punk movement was a time of great social insecurity.

That said, for many of us who grew up in the punk community, it was primarily positive, a safe place to express one's anger and hurt and fear: whether playing guitar or screaming lyrics or slam dancing, I felt safe to be me. Even diving from a stage, I expected the crowd to catch me to pass me around. It's the ultimate version of those trust exercises you hear about in team-building exercises: how I'd use a monitor speaker for more lift, take to the air some five feet above people's heads. I'd turn so my back was to them lifting my booted-feet up to make sure I didn't kick anyone in the head. Mutual trust: I will try not to hurt you, you will try to make sure I don't get hurt. There was a rule of receptivity, too: when I was on the dance floor, I caught whomever jumped next. I remember doing this ten times during a DOA set at the old Rock Hotel on Jane Street. It didn't matter how obnoxious my behavior was, I was caught, surfed the crowd.

It would be another dozen years before DOA covered "It's Not Unusual."

DOA is a band that embodies the positive aspects of punk, with their simple equation of Talk-Action=0. You have to work to make a change, to be your best self, you need to act. If you want to change the world or yourself, nihilism isn't enough. It takes action. You must aspire.

And that action could be rooted in positivity. It was on the scene that I first heard the concept of PMA. The all-Black hardcore band the Bad Brains preached the idea of keeping a Positive Mental Attitude, reminding us "Don't care what they may do/We got that attitude!" How important it was—how important it is—to stay positive, even when things seem tough. Stay together.

THIS ISN'T TO SAY IT'S EASY TO KEEP ONE'S PMA, ESPECIALLY IN THE FACE of adversity. And daily living can be adverse. I've been there: bouncing at a bar at night after graduate classes, then waking up early with my infant son. Then off to teach my sections of Freshman comp at Western Michigan University. I often didn't have a babysitter: young Alex would come to Sprau Tower with me and usually a fellow grad student might watch him for an hour. Though once I returned from class and couldn't find Alex anywhere. I panicked, I admit. As I ran down the two flights of stairs to the main department offices. And there he was asleep in the English Department chair's office.

Despite the hardships of that time: not making enough money to pay for rent, food, diapers, the car necessary to live in Kalamazoo, and utilities, I lived in a supportive community. The people there—the professors who took me out to eat or hired me for odd jobs, the former students or bar patrons who worked in restaurants and often charged me for just a cup of coffee, the pediatrician who once said after an emergency visit to the office on a Friday night that "this visit didn't happen"—helped mitigate hardship. That's what good community does. In interviews I've read with gang bangers, union workers, and punks, in discussions I've had with girl scout leaders, choir singers, and students in MFA programs one thing stands out, they all say what they like about being in the group is that they felt like they belonged. In the communities of punk rock, in the community of poets, in my arts community of friends today, and in those days in Kalamazoo, when I belonged to the community of the MFA program and Club Soda, I felt like I belonged.

Some days, though, when I spent my last dollars for the week on Wednesday on diapers and baby food, and realized I had little to eat but peanut butter and bread until the next payday, it was easy to despair, to feel the difficulty of my situation, to even, briefly obsess about it. Trouble comes. It can be hard to stay positive.

STILL, NO FOOD HAS ARRIVED. I TRY TO REMIND MYSELF THE IMPORTANCE of patience. The food won't show up any sooner if I'm frustrated. Neither will happiness.

We have the right to pursue happiness in the United States. If this doesn't come at the expense of other people, then this right is tantamount to how we live. Should people want to marry someone of the same gender they should be able to do it because their individual happiness is what matters. They have the right to pursue it. Their happiness—their private choices—have no bearing on my capacity for my own happiness. If they want to bless me in the words of their choosing, why should I look to be aggrieved, aggravated, agitated.

When otherness threatens someone else's security, the response is fear. That's not on the gay couple or the person wishing us a happy holiday, that's on the threatened self that reacts (reflex) rather than responds (reflects). In my dealings with my closest relations, when someone wants to deliver bad news or tell me something I don't like, I often say, "I'm going to react first. Please ignore the reaction. Then I will respond." The reaction is impulse, it is not mediated. Responses are mediated. To live fully in the world with another person one must be able to do both mindfully.

Sometimes it's as is if people think there's a limited amount of happiness in the world and, if others are happy, they're taking away from our allotted stock of happiness, like Cabbage Patch Kids before Christmas in 1983. Parents fought each other for the dolls reinforcing the notion that the Cabbage Patch Doll would make their child happy. Fortunately, there's no limited supply of happiness. To be angered by and complain about the happiness of others will not make us any better off; we cannot grab one side of the happiness box from the hands of another, and tug it, duke it out, then lift our bedraggled package to the check-out line.

The fact is that capitalism encourages us to want what others have and often inundates us with messages suggesting *supplies are limited so order today.* Evolutionary biology begs us to hoard what we have to survive the winter, to share with our family/ our tribe so the genes perpetuate, and to raid the enemy tribes if it will help us survive. The history of politics is one in which leaders manipulate the sense of otherness, even in a country such as ours, the name of which begs us to not see otherness: "United" States.

The fact is we can't help but see the Joneses. They live right next door. See how they flaunt their successes. See how they smile. See how "happy" they are.

OBVIOUSLY, THEY'VE MASS PRODUCED THIS PRINT OF THE RUBBER DUCK, with its large eyes in its yellow head, the orange beak curved into a smile. It watches like a portrait of the Buddha. I think to name it Friday, after Crusoe's companion. Think to name it *Endurance*. Neither sticks.

What is it that led me to those stories of seafaring? Even *Star Trek* was just a ship on the oceans of space. One summer, I read both *Treasure Island* and *Robinson Crusoe* in the same summer, so that for years I forgot it was Defoe who wrote the latter. If you asked me in my twenties or thirties, I would have insisted it Stevenson authored Crusoe.

I think now to name the duck Gulliver, because I read Swift, too. And the duck is so large, a Brobdignarian bath toy.

I don't know who invented the rubber duck. I don't know who opted to take this portrait and blow it up poster size, but I imagine they were whimsical in a way I'd particularly like. I imagine they're happy if only because of what Robert Louis Stevenson said: "There is no duty we so much underrate as the duty of being happy. By being happy we sow anonymous benefits upon the world." This portrait is one of those anonymous benefits.

"The secret of happiness, you see, is not found in seeking more, but in developing the capacity to enjoy less." —Socrates

This inherent truth about happiness functions in opposition to Capitalist dictums. Christ said give away what you have and follow him, but people subscribe to a prosperity Gospel of multimillionaire ministers. None of the disciples did that well: they met their ends, more often than not poor and alone but believing themselves righteous, good, even if the Romans and the Pharisees condemned them.

My gay friends who lost their families coming out of the closet for admitting who they were created communities that have shared values, shared love. And yet I know their sadnesses: one admits he misses his parents, another wept when not welcome to her father's funeral. They have had to enjoy less but enjoy it more fully, with the complete essence of who they are.

When I was in a relationship with a Jamaican woman, my father wondered why I would make my life so much harder on myself. I hadn't. I loved whom I loved, and was loved back. Unfortunately, it was comments like my father's and similar one's by Shari's brother that made our lives and our loving so much harder, more insecure, more unstable.

That's how we found unhappiness in our relationship.

THERE IS AN EXPRESSION GOING AROUND IN SELF-HELP CIRCLES THAT we are *human beings not human do-ers.* That is to say, that we shouldn't get caught up in our work lives, strive for promotions; we shouldn't take our work home with us if it prevents us from enjoying our families, our friends, our lovers, our pets. But this fails to acknowledge the work we do that brings us joy, those vocations that call to us. Unfortunately, in the United States it's easy to get caught up in work, in making money for some unknown stockholders, in feeling like we have to succeed, to get prestige, maybe a Christmas bonus. Worse, in the corporate climate of the last twenty years, it's easy to feel like not working harder might mean getting fired, laid off, let go.

I love teaching Creative Writing, in part, because the people pursuing their MFAs have chosen to pursue something they love, and many hope to find their happiness in this vocation. In the low residency program, the students are often older: having worked hard for years or having been silenced for years, they are finally given an opportunity to live unmasked. And still, it's scary for them.

Insecurity con contribute to unhappiness. Uncertainty, particularly as it may impact our households, is something we often don't want to talk about so as to keep up appearances. Working harder out of fear is to be insecure. To work for more money to have greater security is to be insecure. It's amazing to see extraordinarily wealthy people who want for nothing not want to increase the minimum wage.

We can't be happy if we fear the rug being pulled out from under us. Anxiety and depression are rampant in part because insecurity is rampant: workplaces are changing becoming more computerized, old industries are failing and new industries are complicated, the social contract that companies and governments maintained with their employees and citizens are breaking down, so pensions disappear and there's less money for social services.

I know this to be true: we can't be happy in insecurity. I lived much of my life insecure: in the rentals we lived in, afraid of being molested again or that my secret would be found out, in my relationships with both my mother and father, in my relationship with my friends. Later, I carried that insecurity with me. I was never good enough. It didn't matter that I was valedictorian, that I was the first in my family to go to graduate school, that I published a book, put out a record, et cetera et cetera. For decades I kept trying to say "I'm good enough" to an audience of none.

Even today, there are days I feel like a fraud, afraid I'll be found out. This isn't about anything I do or have done, but rather the old stuff bubbling up.

"FAKE IT 'TIL YOU MAKE IT," THE SAYING GOES.

Fake it means work at it, like you know what you're doing. Go through the motions, but work at it. Aspire. Process process process.

AND TOO, WE ARE HUMAN DO-ERS. TO IGNORE THAT IS TO IGNORE A fundamental truth of how we exist in the world. My work provides me with a community. The university I teach at establishes a group of people with similar values and goals. My students are part of this community that share a passion for writing and poetry. The workplace is a community, one with a complicated culture and challenges, and also a place where fitting in can be incredibly healing.

For one of my earliest jobs, I was a street messenger for a brokerage company a couple od summers when I was a teenager. Most of the runners as we were called were young men of different backgrounds: two rappers from Brooklyn, a southern runaway, and punk rock me. We quickly became a community. When runs were assigned we'd meet downstairs and re-divide the work because we understood certain banks and brokerage firms' operations in ways the bosses didn't. We identified in opposition, but we were together. We had a culture that was both part of and separate from the greater culture of Josephthal and Company. This has been true of labor for years. No one cared what we looked like. No one cared what we listened to on our Walkman headphones as we walked the streets of the financial district. We were out of the office. Then we'd run our separate ways.

As a teenager and young adult, I made myself more secure by telling lies, by creating a new mask, a Gerry that was more accomplished, more cool, more successful. This was about my own insecurity in my standing. The lies were just moments of hyperbole, making a myth of Gerry. People would like me more if I was more __ *fill in the blank*__. I was convinced, the way many who have been victims of childhood sexual abuse are, that I wasn't good enough for friends, for a girlfriend, for happiness. Of course, this led to a conundrum: what would happen if people found out the truth.

The catch 22: I was faking it 'til I made it, but was setting myself up to never make it. In other words, the very thing that I thought would make me secure was incredibly precarious, was dangerously insecure. More than once, the lies came out and then disaster, which just reaffirmed my sense that I was not good enough.

Shame is nothing if not the manifestation of a kind of insecurity. How can one be happy if one is ashamed?

Shame is what Adam and Eve discovered upon eating the Fruit in Paradise. Caught they tried to lie to god. Getting expelled from Eden was the first moment of insecurity. Banishment, the first punishment.

SOMETIMES I IMAGINE ADAM AND EVE IN THEIR SHAME, LOCKED OUT of paradise. They can see it through the gates, that garden, the better life. How they must have wanted to figure out a way to get the guarding angels drunk, to slip back through the gates. How frustrating! With shame must have come anger. Did Adam berate Eve? Or himself? First betrayed by their desire to be more than they were, then betrayed by their desire to return.

Or consider their sons, how Cain's jealousy of Abel leads him to unhappiness. Consider his rage. It is the manifestation of his unhappiness. Thich Nhat Hahn says, "Jesus did not say that if you are angry with your brother, you will be put in a place called hell. He said that if you are angry with your brother, you are already in hell. Anger is hell." One cannot be happy if one is in hell.

CONSIDER THE EVENTS THAT HAVE MADE US MOST UNHAPPY. How many of those things are associated with an end to security? Our significant other breaks up with us—the security of our relationship is ended. Someone dies—the securities of our community and of our health are called into question. An accident in our driving or a poor decision—the security of our competence is ruined. A sudden bill—our financial security is shaken.

Time and again the things that make us sad or scared are, in some ways, threats to our security. And feeling these things requires they get our attention: it's evolutionary. The wildebeest howling outside is a threat to our security: that we must protect ourselves from it is our first priority.

Ditto, if we consider those things we generally associate with "making us happy," they revolve around events that increase our sense of security. A new job, a new relationship, a windfall, each increases our sense that we are capable, lovable, safe and secure. The act of gift giving is a way of reinforcing the community of friends and family: they embody that security.

B EING A RUNNER WAS A FUN JOB BECAUSE IT ENTAILED simultaneously a lot of freedom and a sense of responsibility. Out on the streets of lower Manhattan, no boss watched over my shoulder, and before the age of cell phones, no one could check in on me. It required commitment and autonomy. It wasn't always easy. Heavy rains (more than once I had to work during hurricane hits) would have me arrive in offices with soaked clothes, wet shoes. Walking the streets in 100-degree days meant I would sweat and be perpetually thirsty. Why wouldn't I want to dip into J&R Music and scan through the records for a half hour just to give me a pause to cool down? Back on a run, receptionists would look askance, reminding me, always that I wasn't part of the office community. All us runners worked downtown, but we weren't of downtown. It was my first job in the service industry, not my last.

When the delivery guy shows up with my Indian food, I will tip 25%. Usually, I tip at the 20-25% range. It's a way of recognizing him and the work he's done for me. How easy it is to forget that the people working in the service industry are serving us: I am blessed by their work, and thus I see the gratuity as a kind of tithing. My brother, a good businessman, thinks this is foolish, but I feel secure in my capacity to tip at that level. I see it as an act not of charity or generosity but of gratitude. If I could, now, I would ask Sister Gertrude why gratitude isn't one of the seven virtues.

AGAIN, LET ME POINT OUT, I SPEAK FROM A PLACE OF PRIVILEGE. I can afford, now, to tip 25%. I'm a white male who, despite lots of obstacles, has had a lot of opportunities. I'm not Caucasian-American. I'm American. One of the ones who doesn't have to hyphenate. The very *act* of hyphenating emphasizes otherness, isolation from, a kind of banishment.

I recognize this. I also recognize that much of what I'm talking about is easier said than done. Many people, as I did in my childhood, live in chronic insecurity. Financial. Emotional. Psychological. I admit sometimes I live with it still. There are times when what I aspire for leads to desires, and once that happens, I'm aware of insecurities. My best friends have heard my petty complaints, my fears, my frustrations. But these are not moments of failure, they are just part of the process. Nonduality. What I've discovered is that by training myself to recognize my abundance, to find my satisfaction in aspiration rather than outcome, I bounce back more quickly, the lows aren't that low.

Gratitude, one key to happiness.

In other words, I reaffirm the things that enhance my sense of security.

And the lows have been low. I have considered suicide more than once and well beyond adolescence. I have felt abandoned and lost.

Nietzsche said, "Happiness is the feeling that power increases—that resistance is being overcome." This often gets confused to mean that this is about power over others, power over nature, power over otherness. But Nietzsche talked about the overman, that man who overcomes, and often the thing we need to overcome most of all is the limitations we put on ourselves, the way we see ourselves, the past we continue harkening to as a way to define our today.

The good old days weren't all that good. And the bad old days were surely bad, but their badness can be overcome if the will is there. For Nietzsche overcoming was about the *will* to power, and our will is ours no one else's. Will is the force of aspiration. And by power, dare I say, he meant the power over ourselves, over our worst tendencies, over our ability to settle for good enough.

BEFORE MY MARRIAGE A FRIEND ASKED ME IF I WERE HAPPY IN MY RELATIONSHIP. We'd been walking together through the woods, she and me, talking about our futures. The mosquitoes buzzed us, and before I could say anything, she said, "Whatever you say, don't tell me you're content. Content is the kiss of death."

I nodded. *Content* was the word I was going to use.

Content, meaning not restless.

Content, a C grade.

Content, meaning "good enough."

It's funny that *content* and **content** are the same words. The fact is I felt content because I wasn't sure about my own content: what it was I was made of at the time. For so long it seemed like something was missing inside of me, and I was looking to fill that space with relationships that often felt like I was settling. I found myself dating women (marrying women!) whom I felt needed me; and that need allowed me to feel useful, provided me with a purpose. I worked hard to fulfill their needs thinking that would satisfy my need to be loved.

The world, of course, isn't that simple. To be needed by someone is not the same thing as being loved by them. And believing in the Karma made me think that being there for someone else's needs meant they would be there when I had needs. We should all know by now that Karma doesn't quite work like that.

IF WE SCRUTINIZE IT, GOOD ENOUGH NEVER LEADS TO SECURITY. My Kirtland students handing in C work because it was good enough were one bad paper away from failing. Good enough only maintains the status quo, which for many is a state of insecurity. A state directly opposed to being happy.

CONUNDRUM: IF ELMER FUDD EVER CAUGHT BUGS BUNNY, would he be happy? Let's face it, if he killed the rabbit, he would go out and hunt another rabbit, wouldn't he? By nature, he's a hunter, therefore hunting is what he does. The catching might satisfy him, it would surely put food on the table for the night, but he'd have to do it again. That's the problem. And the joy.

Every poem finished brings relief. And with it comes a moment of dread in which I fear not knowing how to start a new poem that isn't just a clone of the one I finished.

I taught well earlier. Tomorrow, I'll have to teach again, and I have to try to teach equally well, or better. If I don't, so be it as long as I put the effort in to make it a good class. As with most thing, outside forces such as classroom dynamics, student personalities and energy levels, et cetera, have as much to do with how a lesson goes as what I control. What I gage then is what's in my control: my will and preparation, my trained skills and experience.

It will be about -3 degrees when I leave for campus in the morning, and I can complain about not teaching in the South or in the Caribbean, but really, those places would have their own shortcomings that I just can't see from here.

The window rattles with a wind burst. Someone drives my food here. My son delivered pizzas for a few weeks and hated it; my nephew delivered Chinese food and enjoyed it. They both have gone on toward their individual futures. For many, I know, delivering food isn't a transitional job, but the livelihood they have. It's unsatisfying, perhaps. It offers no purpose. It requires the driver to deal with frustrated hungry people, too lazy or privileged to go out on a night like this one. I'm guilty as charged.

I had a friend who was a life-long waiter. He said, for him, a man who loved food and people but didn't have the skills necessary to cook, that waiting tables was the best job he could imagine: he brought people their meals and got to watch them enjoy it. Sure, he had some bad experiences with customers and he sometimes saw people do cruel things (seeing break-ups happen at the restaurant table made him give free desserts to the heartbroken; it was the only consolation he could imagine from his position), but more often than not he saw people's joy. It paid the bills, he said. It was noble work.

NOTHING IS THIS SIMPLE. NO DICHOTOMY MEANS THAT THE SELF AND the outside world are one. My work life affects my happiness. The weather can affect my happiness (ask anyone with seasonal affective disorder!). My body lives in the world of stimuli: a rotten piece of fruit will make me spit it out, a bad smell will make me cover my nose; I've sat through many a fine meal that I couldn't enjoy because the restaurant was too loud or too cold or the chairs uncomfortable. All of these things are disappointments, frustrations, aggravations. Like a skyscraper in a storm, my mood swayed, but the architecture of happiness is such it is designed to sway. Although the skyscraper isn't part of the natural world, it must be built with an understanding of geophysical realities. Without such design, they would fall over.

No person, not even the Dalai Lama, is impervious to negative stimuli. The goal becomes to cultivate a foundation that allows you not to make the negative stimuli personal. The loud restaurant isn't being done to you; it is a fact. The rotten fruit wasn't deliberately given to you. Someone might bite into a bad apple and say, "Just my luck. This *always* happens to me," and thereby create an identity of victimhood and identify themselves with the bad fruit. The bad fruit can ruin their day.

This is not to delegitimize the effects of ingrained poverty, institutional racism and sexism, and the stigmatization of those who live outside of cultural norms. No dichotomy means each of us exists as part of our culture/history and it is part of us. The latter part is the force within us that can change (albeit slowly) the communities we live in, be it the familial culture that wishes we'd have children when we don't want to, the religious culture that attempts to deligitimize religious plurality by claiming "happy holidays" is part of a war on Christmas, or a police department that stigmatizes blackness. All of these things attempt to devalue individuality and creates insecurity in our identity, but finding ways to make peace between ourselves and the mainstream community requires it be as much our job as it is theirs. Fortunately, we can also find comfort in subcultures that share our values and reenforce self-worth at the same time, and we create new "families" with our friends and lovers to develop a new sense of shared values.

A FEW YEARS AGO, A WOMAN I LOVED ENDED OUR RELATIONSHIP. It happened unexpectedly. Only the week before she had joined me in this very hotel actually, in a suite similar to this one, bringing a bottle of prosecco with her. Before that we had spent a week on the road, which culminated in my meeting her best friend and exploring one of the favorite places of her childhood. I'd felt blessed.

A week later: caput.

Most people know what it's like to be devastated by heartache and loss. The security of our relationship vanished suddenly, as if by magic. Worse, we had been such good friends, so much so we often had multiple conversations going via email, text, instant messenger, and in person at the same time, that a cornerstone of my daily life was gone. The shared language of our time together was gone, and all of a sudden, I'd been struck mute. I felt more lost than I'd felt in a long time. The community of my relationship had vanished, and more, I didn't want to talk about it with people in my other communities. Banished, I was ashamed and heartbroken. Whatever dysfunction plagued our relationship might have been worked on, but instead I felt enveloped by insecurity. I couldn't sleep, and it took until about six weeks into this new life for my then 23-year-old son came upstairs from his basement room to say he was worried about me. It was a little after four in the morning. He'd been listening to me pace above him every night for forty days, the floorboards below me, creaking his ceiling. His lack of understanding just emphasized my isolation.

Three weeks later I flew to one of the most beautiful places in the world: Florianopolis, Brazil. The greens in the Parque du Sol across from my hotel glowed, verdant and vibrant despite the fact that it was autumn in the southern hemisphere. Lush was a word I welcomed. People played acoustic guitar there; kids kicked a soccer ball, and their laughter gathered in the leaves of the trees around their field. There was a sky full of new-to-me constellations. I didn't speak Portuguese, so I had to focus on the language in order to pick up phrases, find people willing and able to speak English. There were many such people, strangers who bought me drinks, asked me about the U.S., introduced me to their friends. I felt welcome into this community, and I luxuriated in it. I laughed a lot. I returned to my hotel each day, both exhausted and exhilarated, and although my lost companion had originally planned to accompany me, and although I missed her and wanted to recount each adventure to her, I slept through each night. I was out of my day-to-day life. I continued to be heartbroken, but I couldn't obsess about heartache. I had lectures to give about Elizabeth Bishop at universities, and afterward I'd read poems to students or else talk about pop culture,

At the end of the week, I stood with a former student at his wedding on the beach. My grief was not welcome here. It wasn't gone. It just wasn't acceptable. So much beckoned for my attention. So much was saying, *enjoy enjoy enjoy.*

Ironically, being out of my community led me out of exile.

When I returned to the States, I had a new story to tell. One not of shame but of triumph.

LOOKING BACK AT THAT WEEK IN BRAZIL, I RECOGNIZE THAT PART of what mitigated my sense of loss had to do with the fact that I was there doing things that made me secure. I spoke to students of all different ages about subjects I love; I read poems, and in poetry I have always felt at home, felt like I was my best self.

I also had left behind all the things that reaffirmed my loss, my grief, my feeling that this loss was some sort of reflection of my shortcomings—what I think of as a knee jerk reliance on shame that I've had since childhood—and I was forced to pay attention to this world around me. I didn't speak the language, the flora and fauna were all new and so piqued my curiosity, and everyone I met had a strange story, a new insight, an interesting view of the world that I, a good guest, had to give attention to.

The trip's last few days I spent celebrating the marriage of a former student of mine to the daughter of a Brazilian shipbuilding family. Zac had been my student in Michigan, and I hadn't heard from him in several years when the invitation arrived, one of only a few he sent to people in the States, but he wanted me to know I had affected him in important ways. When I told him I planned to attend the wedding, he honored me by asking me to stand with the groomsmen, which I gladly did.

Being with Zac, being appreciated by him in this way, reminded me of the communion I make with students, how much teaching matters, how much security I get from it. More, though, I am reminded of how much security I received from certain teachers and professors. In graduate school in particular, when I was often single-dadding my way through class, when economic insecurity was an everyday part of my life, certain professors hired me to work for them, keeping me in dinners and Alex in diapers.

MORE: I HAD A VISION FOR AN OUTCOME FOR OUR RELATIONSHIP, one, in the end, she didn't share. I desired a particular life. I aspired to be a good partner. I drove to New York from Frostburg every other week; I paid rent for an apartment there I rarely slept in, I listened and advised and asked for advice. Still, I know I had my shortcomings, and the relationship had its shortcomings. Like many partners, we reveled in our shared otherness; we were isolated but not alone; in my fantasy, we were a literary Bonnie and Clyde with pens rather than Tommy Guns. Despite our partnership, we were not equals: socio-economically and experientially we were different. Her parents, with whom she was estranged, were keenly wary of our relationship, and keenly aware of their own status. We made them insecure: I was many things that they didn't want for her daughter, and in the end, our relationship rubbed against the expectations and desires she was raised with.

Her father once asked her what shortcomings I had that I still played punk rock, still played in a band. For him it was an act of immaturity. It was a way of criticizing me while simultaneously questioning my relationship with his daughter, many years my junior.

No one ever asked, when I was one of two adults playing basketball for fun, why I was playing a game. If I were playing jazz or singing in a choir, I'm sure he wouldn't have asked the question. It had to do with the type of music I was playing. If he'd asked me (he was much too polite for that sort of thing), I would have told him I play punk rock for the same reason I play basketball: I like the physical activity, the social engagement, the sense of play and the sense of work combined in the same activity. It gives me joy. I would have said something similar about why I chose to spend so much time with his daughter. In the end though what I aspired to do and what I desired were not in alignment. This is about ends and means.

THE ENDS JUSTIFY THE MEANS, THE SAYING GOES: THAT PUTS DESIRED outcome over everything else. I've read *The Prince*. I've watched the unfolding of the Trump presidency and US politics in general. My own actions in the past have been driven at times by my own desires for people to perceive me a certain way, to not disappoint anyone, to stabilize some sense of insecurity that is deep-rooted.

Why do we act how we act?

Over an hour since my order, and still no goat vindaloo. Some would say I shouldn't tip him, but I maintain my commitment to 25%. It both does and doesn't feel generous. I've tipped so generously at times that my credit card company has called to ask whether the tip had been forged. And I tell you this not to gloat or have you go, "What a great fellow," but to create a context for the following discussion. Why do I tip well, why should anyone tip well? Here's where desire and aspire come into play.

I could tip well because I want people to see me as generous (see above). On a date, I might tip well so the woman I'm with will think, *wow, what a giving guy*. That's desire. I want to control how someone sees me. In this case, though, I will never see the driver again, and there's no one to impress. More, to the best of my ability to do so, I'm done trying to impress anyone. Having the esteem of others might make me feel good, but that's not happiness, just the appeasement of insecurity.

I could tip well because I feel guilty for how often I was too poor to tip well, and I want to make up for it. Perhaps we can argue this is more noble than the first scenario, but the source of this behavior remains some insecurity, action rooted not in my own stability but in the crumbling foundation below my feet.

Some people tip well because they pity the server or "feel bad" for him/her.

Kant says the morality of the deed has to do with the motivation behind it. We can't treat people as a means to an end: all of the above scenarios treat the driver like a prop: the money given to him to appease something in me.

The driver has done me a service, a service he gets paid for. That's an argument to not tip. But he's also done me a favor, made my life easier in some way; tonight, it was that he kept me from going outside in the bitter cold, and he brought me food, even late. I tip out of gratitude: he is my equal and I am grateful for his help. It is a private exchange between he and myself. I aspire to honor his work by sharing a little of what my own work has afforded me.

I'm happy to be able to do it.

In a shadow box in my office at home is, among other things, a postcard a Buddhist monk on the streets gave me once. It says "May you be happy. May you be peaceful."

After my relationship with L ended, I felt unmoored, unstable, insecure, so I dated several women, unable to commit to any; hurting them, myself and leading to all sorts of conflict. One asked me what I wanted, a perfectly reasonable question. She, of course, wanted specifics, but I went abstract as is my wont. "I want peace," I said.

Peace is essential to happiness. Peace is a type of security.

In the Catholic Church growing up, the offering of peace: a handshake with the people sitting close to you, was an essential part of each mass. It exists to establish a sense of community, a sense that these are my people, a sense of stability. Jesus offered peace to renegades and misfits who chose to question the accepted cultures of Rome and Judaism at the time; he offered security. Be who you are and I love you, Jesus said.

That's not the philosophy I experienced in Catholic high school mind you, particularly in the early 1980s in Staten Island, New York. There, nonconformity was met with scorn on good days, random acts of violence on others. Once, I was sucker punched in the throat as I walked down a flight of stairs. A non-conformist must be confronted, the theory goes, because nonconformity is a threat to stability.

Christians became Rome. Rock 'n' roll, punk, rap all become main stream. Homosexual marriage becomes the law. Culturally, such assimilation reasserts a sense of security (though history shows us that when a culture feels insecure, it may turn upon those it assimilated). Jesus offered a new community founded on loving thy neighbor, on peace and security. The Founding Fathers offered a security based on community, on "We the people …" on being a united community of states.

Reading social media today, it can be hard to find that unity. Headlines and clickbait are designed to make us feel at times afraid. Perhaps that's why people are less happy, they're less secure.

Despite this, I think to take a break and check my social media feeds.

HAPPINESS IS A CHOICE, THE OLD SAYING GOES. I DON'T DISAGREE, but I don't agree.

Nonduality.

In grade school, Ms. Cox, the science teacher at St. Charles Elementary, taught that everything was made of atoms, and that atoms had three component pieces: the positively charged proton, the negatively charged electron, and the neutrally charged neutron. Every atom had the same number of neutrons as protons.

We are composed of atoms; therefore, we must have similarly balanced number of positively charged particles and negatively charged particles. Positive feelings and negative feelings. We must, also, have neutral particles, times in which we are neither feeling positive or negative. Those times might feel "negative" because they have none of the charge (literally) of the positive atoms. They aren't. Accept neutrality for what it truly is.

Or to put it another way: my experiences of grief, of loss, of general sadness help define the contours of my feelings of pleasure, of joy, of "happiness." We cannot have one without the other. If we never feel that rumbling in our stomach that defines "hunger" or the bloated feeling of being full, how would we know the satisfaction of having eaten? I wonder where the food delivery person is, and have a rush of aggravation that I recognize because it offsets the joy of writing these passages. All feelings exist insofar as they have equally important and necessary counter that helps define their contours. But there are days—most days, if I'm honest—when neither the extreme of joy or the extreme of despair exist. So much exists between the poles.

In a recent interview in the *New York Times*, Philip Roth says this about writing: "Exhilaration and groaning. Frustration and freedom. Inspiration and uncertainty. Abundance and emptiness. Blazing forth and muddling through. The day-by-day repertoire of oscillating dualities that any talent withstands—and tremendous solitude, too."

Oscillating dualities is the same thing as nonduality.

Like Roth, I've struggled with the blank page and the well inked page; I've felt excited trepidation with the words as they came. Really though, it's not just in my writing life: I live like that in everything I do. The writing life is a microcosm of my actual life, chock full of inspiration and uncertainty. Abundance and emptiness.

For some it's that they were out in the great stretch of the outdoors with all that it entails in search of mushrooms, and found none.

I've ordered dinner. It hasn't yet come.

SOME PEOPLE TALK ABOUT HAPPINESS AS IF IT'S A DESTINATION. Ask MapQuest or Google Maps to get you to happiness and see what happens. You can't go three and a half miles and make a right and get to happiness. You don't go three hundred miles either. There's no treasure map to happiness, no X marking the spot. As a matter of fact, if you keep hunting it, it's going to keep eluding you, that wascally wabbit.

Or think of it the way Stephen Dunn put it in his poem "Happiness":

A state you must dare not enter
with hopes of staying...

In Florianapolis, I allowed myself to be happy in part because I was away from my troubles, away from heartache, away from the reminders of my unhappiness. I was also away from the bills in the mail, the day-to-day requirements of being a professor (for it was spring break), the household chores, the daily demands of being at home. I was re-secured in some essentials of my being. *If only I could live here*, crossed my mind a few times as I strolled along the beach or walked along the Beira mar Norte or drank a caipirhina and watched the rains come in.

Well, in order to do that, I'd have to get a job that provided security to pay all my expenses, find a place to live that would come with a series of chores, be there not only when the weather was beautiful and beachy every day, but make it through a winter in the southern hemisphere. The reverie would be replaced by the mundane, and by whatever insecurities might come with being a foreign national living and working in Brazil. In other words, in those states of both Brazil and happiness, my time was temporary.

ERNEST SHACKLETON MADE SEVERAL EXPEDITIONS TO ANTARCTICA. He'd hoped to be the first person to reach the South Pole, but even when he failed and others beat him there, he continued to want to reach the Pole. He lived and sailed at the end of the great age of Exploration in the early 20th century. His ship, The Endurance, got locked among the ice floes, inevitably got smashed by the ice, and he and his crew survived as best they could, having to eat penguins and seals and eventually, even the sled dogs, having to give up so much of the things they cherished that they had brought on the ship as they moved onward to survive.

One of the things Shackleton gave up was the trappings of "command." He was still the captain, but the hierarchy of British naval rules didn't make sense at the bottom of the world, freezing and hungry. What made sense was survival. He recognized was that the men needed their morale kept up. Having their captain be one of them, helped with that. More it lessened his own isolation as an officer alone. After their basic needs of food, water, shelter, their morale—that sense of cheerfulness, confidence, and zeal— became crucial to survival. Ditto, he understood they all needed a sense of purpose, a job to do, a role in the community. Without such things there is no hope. Hope is a big part of happiness.

Consider how the linguistic roots of *happiness* and *hope* are the same. They derive from *hap*, which is the Old Norse and Old English word for luck. When you're lucky you are happy. When you want to be lucky, you have hope.

We don't talk about things like morale anymore. We have businesses that fire people and give their presidents multimillion dollar bonuses, not thinking of how it might create insecurity among the work force. Insecurity is bad for morale. Bad employee morale is bad for business and bad for profit. Morale must be an aspect of happiness. Morale must be a sign of hope.

How important was the community of the Endurance? The establishment of roles and responsibilities, that camaraderie, the sense of shared values and shared adventure; of shared possibility and shared loss? It was as much the thought of his men as it was his family in England, and the promise to King and Country that led to all of them surviving. They worked together and when one couldn't work because of illness they worked for him. Shipmates are a family, bound together, by shared values, shared commitment, shared goals, and shared quarters: what develops is love. As Khalil Gibran reminds us "Work is love made visible."

OUTSIDE, IT ISN'T ANTARCTIC COLD, AND I AM, FORTUNATELY, IN MY SUITE. Frozen sea water doesn't press against the walls, crack the timbers. I can imagine the sound of that splitting, part scream part siren. I am neither at risk of freezing nor starving to death, so I have it much better than Shackleton and his men. I'm waiting on Indian food not seal blubber or the last of the sled dog steaks. Despite this, I hope the dinner gets delivered soon. I hope the delivery guy's car didn't break down or worse yet, hope that he wasn't in an accident or that he didn't accidentally deliver my dinner to someone else.

Is it any wonder, as cold as it is, that I'm thinking of Shackleton, whom I first read about that 23 below winter day in Roscommon. His story fascinates me, and how could it not? Not only did none of his men die, but how he managed to keep them all alive had to do with how he led, throwing out the top-down hierarchy necessary onboard a normal navy ship in normal waters and in normal times. Shaken by insecurity, the ship's society needed a new community structure.

Despite this, he was considered a failure. After all, he didn't achieve his goal. But to those hapless men stranded, fighting frostbite, killing seals for food, melting snow for water, living with the risk of scurvy, his actions were heroic.

We have made our lives much easier. We have filled our experiences with convenience and entertainment, so that the internet going down feels like we're trapped in the ice floes. We can almost hear the creaking boards, the ice crushing the hull.

I love that his ship was named *The HMS Endurance*: surely our capacity to endure is rooted in our capacity to hope. Ditto, our capacity for happiness is equal to our capacity to do just that.

WIND YOWL GROWS LOUDER AND MORE INTENSE. IT BATTERS THE WINDOWS. It's the same wind Shackleton and his men heard a century ago, it's the same wind that taunted them each long Antarctic night, that carried the voices of no one to Crusoe, that carries Christmas carols every December, carries every *happy holidays* ever proclaimed. It's the same wind that blows through my hair in the MG, the same wind the blew through my hair riding that bike forty years ago. The same wind I'd hear out a different window, ashamed that I chose to take a mouthful of cock rather than a knife blade; ashamed of some lie told to cover up my infidelity or ashamed of the infidelity itself. The wind that would tell of a storm coming.

We had better be prepared, batten down the hatches, board up the windows, secure the perimeter.

The wind howls like the muezzin, calling the faithful to prayer.

God exists in the wind, magnificent and terrible. How long did I live believing "And the Lord will by no means leave the guilty unpunished. In whirlwind and storm is His way"?

And the wind continues: "from heaven a noise like a violent rushing wind, and it filled the whole house where they were sitting." This last bit is from the Acts of the Apostles: imagine those disciples after Christ's death: how scared they must have been, how insecure, how unhappy to have lost him. For them, in the resurrection was hope and security grounded in communion.

I DON'T SUGGEST THE MEN ON THE ENDURANCE WERE HAPPY ABOUT their circumstances. Shackleton's diaries of the trip are full of doubt and self-recrimination as much as they are of duty and hope. He had to choose to keep the men as secure as possible. Even when it meant abandoning the ship and pulling the rescue boats by sledge, even when it meant taking incredible risks that, fortunately, paid off.

The men and he were miserable: they not only missed their wives and families, but more, they suffered greatly: hunger so bad they ate dog meat, a cold that led to frostbite, thirst. The possibility of death loomed everywhere, hiding in the shadows of those 23-hour nights. They knew, after a certain point, their families must have thought them all dead. There was no way to communicate with home: they were removed from every community but this one of the Endurance, and it was not even on shaking ground, but on ice.

The men read the Bible out loud, they read the great books some had packed, Dickens, Tolstoy, Melville, Defoe; they told stories, they kept their community when any others might have mutinied. What is a mutiny but a belief in the insecurity of leadership, and the fracturing of the communion of sailors? By keeping the men secure, by holding that community together, Shackleton assured everyone's survival, their future reunions with loved ones, their sense of happiness, and he did this by recognizing the community of the Endurance in that moment, was no longer the community of the Royal Navy: the barrier between officers and enlisted men needed to be broken down, and the immediate needs of the community had to take priority. Tolstoy wrote, "Man finds happiness only in serving his neighbor. And he finds it here because in rendering service to his neighbor, he is in communion with the divine spirit that lives within them." It's what kept them alive.

In times of great unhappiness, dare I say it, my communities kept me alive. They provided hope.

I REMAINED UNHAPPY IN THE WAKE OF THAT RELATIONSHIP'S END, and even after I returned from Brazil, the awareness that I lived without one of my primary communities led to my making a cascading series of poor decisions. Before it, I believed I was happy in that way as a child I believed we were middle class: it required an imagination that made a trip to Burger King a big deal. It was a big deal to me. And like that, I made do. It also led to some revaluations of my friendships. One thing I promised myself was that I would maintain better communication between my friends and myself, working to ensure I called people more regularly for the contact of voice, beginning a series of irregularly scheduled whiskey afternoons with a friend, and reestablishing connections with people whom I missed. Some of these friends were writers, some musicians, some other professors, some old friends in business and the arts communities. They provided a place of comfort, a place of peace, a place of shared values. More, I had to recommit myself to the classroom, the community of writers, the band, and family. In my despair I found stable ground for a new foundation.

I AM IN PITTSBURGH TO BE PART OF THE CARLOW UNIVERSITY MFA COMMUNITY. The teaching is a joy, the paycheck, a help, but the community of diverse writers from all over the world, from different backgrounds, at different stages of their career coming together with a shared sense of values and ambitions is what gratifies. The students range from recent college graduates to retirees, but they interact fluidly with respect and good nature: they have a cultural connection that is fostered by the program and the University and each other. By taking their work seriously, the students say to each other, *you're valued; what you do matters.* The faculty reinforce this notion.

Despite this, how easily some refuse to buy into the culture of a program, any program. When I arrived at my own graduate program at Western Michigan University, I wasn't prepared for the cultural differences between a small liberal arts college and a major State University, wasn't prepared for the cultural differences between New York City and Kalamazoo. It took me six months to adjust; learning to teach my freshmen students, falling in love, and forming a ska band all created communities that reaffirmed my sense of purpose.

I try to remember this when I see students in the Carlow program struggling: perhaps they are trying to write genre fiction or performance poetry in a workshop geared toward literary fiction or lyric poems. More though, the biggest source of student frustration in programs tends to come from the program not meeting their expectations, what they desired to get from the program or course. My expectations for what a poetry program should be were rooted in my undergraduate experiences at Sarah Lawrence, that Western Michigan University's MFA program didn't, at first, live up to those expectations says more about my desire than it does about the MFA program.

I've come to Pittsburgh in January. If I'd expected it to be balmy, I would have packed the wrong clothes. That would not have been the city's fault or Carlow's fault but my own for having the wrong expectations. The fact is,

I had faculty with whom I could talk to, which helped make me part of the community, but more helped me adjust my expectations and develop a sense of purpose for the poems I would write. When working with my students, I attempt to do the same thing.

THE SNOW OUT THE WINDOW TWIRLS AND VANISHES AS THE WIND BLOWS. The flakes transform, become lit up crystals in the darkness, light cast from the windows and the hotel's outside lighting. The snow and ice so similar to what I saw in northern Michigan, what Shackleton must have seen outside the Endurance. Only the circumstances differ.

Legend has it the Inuit have numerous words for snow: they recognize nuances in the types of precipitation. Franz Boas noted "aqilokoq" for "softly falling snow" and "piegnartoq" for a "snow good for driving sled" as examples. Language helps define and refine experience. Consider the words we have for happiness. Words and how we use them define in part our relationship to community. My life as a poet demands I study how language works and explore the possibilities hidden therein. Often that leads to discovering what's not possible.

More important than our words for happiness, I think, is our words for states of being. In English we either are or aren't something. There's no nuance, no temporality, no sense of what is intrinsic and what is temporary. Compare it to Portuguese (or any Romance language) where there are two forms of the verb "to be." The verb *ser* implies permanence. The verb *estar* temporality.

More often than not, when we speak in English about being happy, we're talking about our momentary self. We are happy right now, which might be something more akin to pleasure or joy. That's very different than being intrinsically happy, where the happy sensation is part of who we are. I can be a happy person who feels sad today. I can be a sad person who feels happy to day. English doesn't provide us the short hand that Portuguese and Spanish do. This is one of the shortcomings of English. This evening, I'm cold. But I'm not a cold person. It's snowing, but the snow will stop. I'm happy.

I AM ALSO HUNGRY, FOR WHICH I WOULD USE *ESTAR* AS WELL. IT'S TEMPORARY. It has been more than 90 minutes since I ordered dinner; it is about 60 minutes later than expected and still nothing. I have gone from mildly hungry to famished, and I am avoiding the container of cashews I've brought with me. My hunger distracts me. I am not thinking "If the delivery guy shows up, I will be so happy," but I am annoyed. I do think, "If the delivery guy shows up, I will get to eat." My happy quotient won't change. I will be grateful. I will be relieved that someone else isn't eating my dinner with gusto in his hotel room, but my happiness won't change.

My expectations, of course, on a somewhat speedy delivery, were established by my understanding with the restaurant and GrubHub. I could be frustrated. That said, I could also have had to go out in this weather, started my car, found a parking space by the restaurant, walked through the -15-degree wind chill to get to its door, and then do it all back again. Based on these choices, I chose to call for delivery. I have to accept that I can do nothing but wait.

When Josh from GrubHub finally arrives, I meet him downstairs. Snow decorates his thick hat. The restaurant had given him the wrong order and when he returned it was cold and they had to recook everything. Then he'd gotten lost. He is apologetic and seems to expect me to be apoplectic. I thank him and return to my room. I have set the table for one—and now I put my rice and goat vindaloo on the plate, add the vegetable pakoras, and rip some garlic nan and bite into it. Surprisingly, the food is still warm, and the sauce is the color of the robes the monks wore at the Tibetan Center in Staten Island wore when I sat with them. They tell me to slow down, but I eat my first few bites quickly, not savoring the taste. The flavors blur together. I get the heat from the vindaloo, the tang of the garlic, the coolness of the mint chutney I've dipped my pakora in, but they're without definition.

This is what I wanted to avoid.

I remind myself to slow down. Enjoy sucking some goat meat from a spur of bone until a whistling intake of air ensues me there's no meat left. The garlic is heavy on the nan, warm in my mouth. I dip some of the bread in mango chutney, to get some sweetness into the mix. I chew and pause. Breathe in the scent. The rice has absorbed some of the vindaloo sauce, and has become bright yellow, almost the color of marigolds.

WE SPEAK OF UNHAPPINESS AS A KIND OF DARKNESS, AND HAPPINESS as a kind of light. It's early January in the northern hemisphere: we are still in the "short" days of the year, only two weeks since the solstice. We know seasonal affective disorder is a thing: sadness lurks in the shadows. Imagine Shackleton and his men marooned during the Antarctic darkness in late June, how those days when sunlight began to reappear, first as a just a dull haze and then slowly as more and more actual light, must have provided possibility, an awareness that any opportunity to escape the ice loomed.

This is how we exist in the darkest times. We scan the horizon. We seek signs of sunlight. Tomorrow, the forecast assures me, the sun will rise a minute earlier than it did today. It will set a minute later. It doesn't seem like much, especially when the high temperature is set to be only 13 degrees. I remind myself it might be higher because weatherman are often wrong.

That little voice, the pessimist in side of me, that contrarian, says, *They could be wrong: it could be colder.* Yes, that's true. I can imagine the ways tomorrow could be worse than today, but I choose not to listen to that voice.

I think of an old punk friend who used to say, "Smile, things could get worse. So, I smiled, and things got worse." He always said it with the same sardonic humor, a kind of chuckle that said something true about human nature. We grin and bear it, as the saying goes. The important part is the grinning.

THE IDEA THAT I MIGHT WRITE A TREATISE ON HAPPINESS, THAT I might have some wisdom to impart, that I might have something to say on this subject might seem arrogant. I should have humility the nuns would say. Humility: noun, meaning "a modest or low view of one's own importance; humbleness." I don't think I know anything more than anybody else. I don't think I know any less, either.

The fact is I spent much of my life feeling almost chronically sad in ways no one would suspect, and now I no longer do. What I'm writing here is what works for me. And it is part of the work of being happy. I am not Boddhisatva. I do not suggest it will work for everyone else, or anyone else, for that matter. That said, I do believe that Boddhisatva exist: they look out for us in very real and practical ways, those mentors who guide us.

In his essay "Nuts and Bolts" from his book on writing poetry, *The Triggering Town,* Richard Hugo writes: "That's what these are. Nuts and bolts. My nuts and bolts. For me they helped, or once helped, and some still do. I'm stating them as rules, but of course they are no more than suggestions—I find the axiomatic tone better to a lot of qualifiers. If these work for you, great."

Hugo was a Boddhisatva for my writing.

These are my nuts and bolts.

The fact is "suffering exists." The fact is failure exists. The fact is abuses of power exist. Ditto hate. Ditto sadness. Ditto desire. We can expect more from our partners, our parents, our friends, our elected officials, the police, our workplaces, or our delivery people, but they, like each of us, are flawed. We must work together to help build inclusive cultures that help create and sustain our own sense of purpose. We will not always succeed.

The fact is if I flip a coin, and you say *heads*, there's fifty percent chance it's going to be heads. On the other hand, there's a fifty percent chance it'll be tails. The question is how do we minimize the suffering, the sadnesses, the desires. For me, I look for the joys, the way sailors looked for the north star by which to sail: even though the waters are cold, the nights long, and we're hungry and suffering at sea, I know how to navigate.

I don't believe like Thoreau that "if you turn your attention to other things, [happiness] will come and sit softly on your shoulder." I do believe you have to tend and cultivate your happiness. Whether I am inspired or not, I have to do the work of writing. Whether I am heartbroken or not, I have to prepare to teach. Whether I am despairing or not, I have to cultivate my joy. Our happiness is our responsibility. It should give us a sense of purpose. It should be what we aspire to, not desire for.

ONE OF THE IMPORTANT THINGS I HAVE LEARNED ABOUT MY OWN WRITING is an understanding of process. As a young poet I would often be concerned when I hadn't written in a few days. I wasn't sure I'd ever be inspired to write another poem. Or that I wouldn't know *how* to write a poem should "inspiration" strike. What I learned over the years was that I couldn't write every day, at least not pen to paper writing; it helped to rethink of writing as a process that required gathering images, thinking about language and relationships, reading, and living a life that provided material for the poems. There was a cycle, of which actually composing poems was only a part of, and not even the first part of. I've met farmers who talk about the importance of winter for the fields, when the work is often just waiting.

I have finally come to realize that joy works similarly. Its process includes moments of non-joy. Times of pensiveness, times of confusion, times of even sadness. Just as I now know that I will write again, even if the feeling of "oh no!" comes to me because I haven't written a new draft in a few weeks, I know that even in times of despair (and despair happens—it can't not happen. Again, nonduality) I will feel joy again.

I try to teach my students that we have to learn their writing cycle. We also have to learn our happiness cycles. Knowing this helps us keep perspective, helps us foster patience, that trickiest of the virtues.

ALL OF THIS IS ABOUT CHOICE. ALL OF THIS IS ABOUT WORK.

I have a student who worries about her love life in part because she doesn't want kids. She identifies herself as other because her family, her friends, all suggest she will want kids. Her sense of not wanting children is permanent, and I believe her. She aspires to not have children. It is a source of anguish for her: she feels out of the mainstream, even though there are any number of women she knows and admires who have chosen to not have children.

Perhaps her parents ask when will she make them a grandparent. Perhaps a friend or a cousin has recently had a baby and can't stop talking about it, and these comments rub up against her insecurities. They help reinforce the idea that her choice is outside the mainstream of the culture that says having children is an important thing. The problem: she wants affirmation—the way so many of us want affirmation—from people whose values don't align with her own. She waits for someone to say "Merry Christmas" to her among people who are saying "Happy holidays." If her parents want her to have children, that says things about their values not hers. More, it says things about their desires, not hers.

More, maybe it says something positive about her, that she has attributes that would make her a good mother, or she has traits that they wish would be passed down. These may be blessings she does not hear. None of those blessings mean she should have children; rather they are affirmations of her own abilities.

More, maybe the idea of being a mother wrecks the security she has, makes her insecure, and thus destabilizes her happiness.

When my son's mother told me she was pregnant, I felt frightened. We were poor graduate students. It'd be a lie to say I was happy about the news. It'd be a lie to say I imagined I would be a great dad: I just planned to be a better father than my own. It'd be a lie to say I was always a good parent, but I did the work of parenting every day.

There was happiness in that. And I learned the joys parenthood provides. I also know not everyone should want or should have children.

I HOPE MY SON LEARNS TO BE HAPPY. HE SUFFERS FROM ANXIETY and bouts of depression the way many young adults do, and like many of my students of that age, sometimes I think he is happiest playing certain video games. Such games involve levels and bosses, and aspiring to do better. Success, of course, fires dopamine, and creates the pleasure of success. Is it any wonder people play them regularly? Video games provide all the pleasures of the real world without any of the physical/emotional risk. Aspiring to a higher level should teach us to aspire in our day-to-day life.

Of course, your character dies in a video game and there's no existential cost. You just reset, start over. More often than not the "real world" doesn't work like that: our hearts get broken, our confidence gets shaken, our body bruised and beaten down. When my son was younger, those things were as much my responsibility as they are now his: that's perhaps the hardest thing about parenting: the responsibility of doing for another, which we haven't always been good at doing for ourselves. It's no wonder parenting is scary: there's no reset button.

That said, even in this endeavor I have the possibility of failure without much risk. Deleted passages, unfinished thoughts, sentences that have been rewritten five or fifty or five hundred times. The process is the point. The process is the pursuit.

WHEN THE WRITING IS GOING WELL, IT ALMOST FEELS EFFORTLESS: one word follows the next, one sentence comes readily after the other. The molecules of phrases made of atomic words, bound together by a quantum mechanics that feels right, natural, instinctual. It almost feels easy. This must be something akin to what athletes call being in "the zone." Playing basketball in Rocsommon, Rich would hit four or five baskets from the three-point range in a row, and he'd be in the zone. My son playing video games, sometimes his instincts are honed and he synchs into the experience and he's in the zone. This is a kind of transcending the body, being part of the bigger thing: ball and court, page, game. This is a kind of ecstasy. It's a great feeling.

Then it ends.

Aristotle says we train ourselves to be excellent at something through practice so that we don't have to be consciously doing, we can just be the experience.

The fact is watching people who are excellent at doing something do it is a kind of joy. Watch a great guitarist play. Watch the Masters (I have no desire to ever golf but to watch a great golfer swing a driver and hit a ball 360 yards spot one is to watch someone who is in tune with nature and movement and their own capacity). Watch an artist at work. Years of process allows this to happen. Years of work.

Then it ends. The next sentence stumbles. A shot gets missed or blocked. And suddenly the athlete it is in slump.

HAPPINESS IS A CYCLE. ITS PEAK IS JOY. WE HAVE BEEN SOLD A BILL OF GOODS, that we can be happy all the time. Not possible; those people who present themselves with constant cheeriness often have a darkness they're running from. I had a student once, an easy-going kid named Eddie, often late, usually smiling. I'd say, "Eddie, you're late" when he arrived to class, and he'd lift his ball cap slightly and grin with a shy sort of embarrassment, then say "Yeah, I know." He was a great presence.

When he hanged himself in the woods behind his family's home, shock and surprise seemed commonplace. "Eddie?" we'd ask in disbelief. He didn't seem unhappy. What does unhappiness look like? Most kids people think of as "being depressed" have outlets for their feelings. They write poems, the draw, they play guitar or drums. They wear black and express their turmoil. They rage against the dying of the light. Often, they will ask me what they should say to their parents when mom and dad ask why they don't write happy poems. I say: "Tell them you're too busy being joyful to stop and write poems at those times." It's good to remind everybody that there's more than just sadness there.

Despite my growth, despite the work (therapy, meditation, a reevaluation of what I value), days still arrive when I feel panicky, alone, sad. Some days, I've returned to an empty house, picked up a book to read, turned on the Stones, and pet the cat: those moments are exactly like many afternoons of my childhood after the assault when I felt anxious and lonesome.

I am not that boy anymore, but that boy remains in my DNA.

Knowing my cycle, I know that these feelings are natural, part of who I am. Just as yesterday's joy is gone, I know that today's sorrow is also fleeting. It only feels like it will last because it is the moment we live in. It's what we have. In today's imagination, the feeling can last forever.

Now I just accept it. I try not to react to it. I respond to it by doing something that I associate with my joy. I pick up the poetry of William Carlos Williams. I plug in a guitar and play it loud. I spin a record and dance "dance naked, grotesquely/ before my mirror/ waving my shirt round my head." I call a friend. I make myself a meal I know I'll enjoy. I am not expecting any of these things to change my mood. My mood is my mood, which is to say my mood is me in the moment, *estar*. I am just reminding myself that my mood is me right now, and my mood is impermanent. I will chip away at it with pleasures Just as earlier in the essay I was hungry, that was me at that moment; now that I've eaten, I've changed that state of being.

OF COURSE, I MAY JUST CHOOSE TO WALLOW IN THE BAD MOOD. That's been known to happen, but even that can be a kind of pleasure.

That said, I keep a list of the things that bring me pleasure. Small things. Things in my control. Things that don't even require me to leave the house. This list is designed to remind me even in the darkest days that there are points of light. My job is to look for them.

ONE OF THE TWO GUYS WHO MOLESTED ME WAS THE SON OF A POLICE OFFICER. Nick was his name: Nick on Emmett Ave, Nick the son of a cop, Nick the son of a bitch, I'd think to myself. He used to knock on the door or window of the apartment we lived in on Buffalo Street. He would demand I open it, let him in. I would go silent, shut the television. I knew to lock the door after I got inside. I was nine. He would tell me that he was going to call the Department of Social Services, the police, the authorities. He said I was too young to be left alone, that I had been abandoned by my mother.

His voice would linger. Sometimes the door knob would turn.

I think of this, sometimes, when I'm home alone. Even in Pittsburgh, even 40 plus years after the fact. The wind rattles the window and it sounds for a moment like him knocking on the glass. I almost expect him to say, "I know you're in there. I know you've been left alone."

People prey on the insecurities of others: politicians do it all the time, peddling fear and a cure for votes. They say, the other is the source of crime, of taking your jobs away, of the variety of hardships facing the country. Peddling fear is a way of peddling unhappiness, it's a reassertion of one's insecurity. This is what Nick was doing, knocking on the door, trying to reinforce my insecurity, compounding my unhappiness, adding fear to shame and loneliness.

In my apartment alone in college, in Kalamazoo, in Roscommon, in Frostburg, in Pittsburgh how have I lived with trace memories of that fear. And how often, too, I have wanted to recreate it because it was something I knew how to survive.

I AM NOT SUGGESTING THAT HEARTBREAK, GRIEF, AND DESPAIR ARE AS EASY to change as being hungry. I'd be a fool to suggest that. Having felt at times like my life was devastated, I understand that it's not easy to "feel better." My life after the assault was broken, but the life I've created from it has value, and I can't imagine who I would be otherwise. My life before I was devastated by heartache was predicated on the notion that my life had value because of a relationship that I was in. What made me unhappy wasn't the break up, but my own co-dependency, my belief that happiness was outside of my being, not inside me. Adam and Eve cast out of paradise thought their happiness was based on the comfort of being in the Garden, not in their community together.

What devastated me was my own doing. It was my desire for a particular type of outcome in my loving that led to hurt. It was my attachment to the relationship that hurt. There is attachment, detachment and non-attachment. There is the difference between desiring and aspiring. Being attached in a relationship can lead, easily to co-dependency. Being detatched can make it seem like we don't care. Non-attached means we care but our selfhood isn't dependent on the relationship.

Which is to say there is a difference between outcome and process. I've known this for years as a writer, but only now, winding through my fifth decade, have I realized this is about living, about loving, about being happy. I aspire that every poem I start will be good. The reality is many won't be. Many will not get beyond a few drafts; many will be mediocre, cover territory formally, subject-wise, rhetorically. Only a few will make me pause, think they are worth keeping. I don't get angry at the poems that fail. The magic is in the process. Ditto: I aspire to be a good person, to do things that fill me with joy, to love well. Relationships will fail, bad things may happen. I have to be focused on process not outcomes.

I AM IN THE IMAGINATION BUSINESS, I TOLD MY BROTHER. We think that the imagination is a good thing, but it can be a monster. My brother has just been diagnosed with prostate cancer and he is a two-time testicular cancer survivor, so he's worried. He's worried, too, about the possible outcomes of surgery: incontinence and loss of sexual function. He's a man in his fifties, why wouldn't he be concerned about these things. They are quality of life concerns. He's been waking up thinking about prostate cancer, about the possible outcomes of coming surgery.

The fact is the imagination is predicated on what we know and what we don't know. It is designed to fill in the blanks, and it is an evolutionary necessity. Our ancestors could imagine how a wild beast might attack them in their sleep and thus could prepare themselves by solving the potential threat. Often, I imagine, some cave person was kept up late at night, night after night, imagining the worst. Someone not getting tenure or talk of firings, can lead me to imagining what's next for the Department of English and my position at the University.

Whatever the threat, whether its our physical health or our emotional health or our professional health, we will imagine the permutations. We will not be able to sleep. The physical toll on us—sleep is crucial to our well-being—will take resources that we need for staying emotionally stable. Insecure, we will feel depressed, sad, overwhelmed. Take away the threat and the imagination has little else to do. Comfort returns.

As a child I took comfort in what was available when I got home from school: Fig Newtons or Chips Ahoy. Reruns of *Gilligan's Island* and *I Dream of Jeanie* and *Star Trek*. My favorite thing to watch then were Looney Toons. Violence and laughter.

Nonduality.

Often there were days when there were no snacks in the kitchen; I might make do with some Saltines, spreading peanut butter on them. Did I watch commercials for Twinkies and Ding Dongs and Hershey bars with a watering mouth? I don't remember doing so. Although in the school cafeteria at lunch, when my classmates pulled out their Hostess cupcakes or their home baked cookies from their cool lunch boxes, I might be painfully aware of how my family lacked such things because the community of my peers watched as I opened the small box of Sun-Maid Raisins my mother packer, on the couch with the crackers and the jar of peanut butter, I was happy to be home with my television, my books, my stereo. No one was there to tease me. It felt somewhat secure.

FUNNY, I TALK ABOUT ELMER FUDD WHEN, PERHAPS, I SHOULD TALK, TOO, about that other *Looney Toons* character, Wile. E. Coyote. He is a creature pure want. Pure desire. For a while, I loved those cartoons, all that ridiculousness, those almost surreal moments. Trains suddenly coming out of painted-on-a-wall tunnels and running over the Coyote, the held moments of the Coyote poised in the air beyond the cliff, how it's not until he looks down that he plummets vanishing into a puff of dust that ascends in his place.

The lesson: desire leads to misfortune.

Imagine if he could give up his desire for the bird, stop picturing it dressed, trussed, roasted and served in his mind, then maybe he would be happier.

But no, he's back again, ACME Instant Tornado Pills at the ready, a bowl of birdseed on the center stripe of the highway.

We all know what happens next. Laughter ensues.

MORE OFTEN THAN NOT, THE AFTERNOONS AFTER SCHOOL REMAINED CALM. My mother might call from work about the child support check, and, if it had come in the mail, she would ask me to walk the six blocks to the bank. How terrified I was on those walks, but how powerless I was to say "no" to my mother. I would have to explain my fear, my rebellion, my refusal, which means I would have to make her face what happened to me, and I didn't want to do that.

I would walk the half block to Amboy Road, and make the right, sticking close to the well populated streets, walking toward the shopping center where the bank was. I thought if I were on well-traveled streets, there would be witnesses. Even so, I imagined, often, Nick showing up, dragging me into a car. Fortunately, traffic might back up behind him, preventing that from happening.

I told myself to be fearless, told myself to do what needed to be done. Isn't that what my mother taught me.

Then he would be there knocking the door. I never felt so abandoned, so insecure. I wanted to be anywhere else, to be anyone else.

I READ BOOKS TO ESCAPE. OPENING A COVER IS LIKE OPENING A DOOR INTO WHATEVER world started on page one. I read fantasy novels and watched science fiction. Is it any wonder I wanted to be Captain Kirk (*Okay, Scotty, beam me out of here*)? Is it any wonder I read and reread *The Hobbit* (I would have rather faced Smaug!)? I loved comic books, too, because I needed a hero, a place where the wrongs of the world got righted by people who only lived in a more perfect moral universe. I played role playing games to live another life, a life in which I was stronger, more capable, and one in which the world was more just.

This is why I started writing, too. One of the worst things to happen to me led me to the thing I love most. It's an inexplicable paradox, but I hear similar things from other writers, artists, musicians, athletes. *I needed to get out of my house. I needed to get out of my head.*

Perhaps the popularity of video games is that it provides and even playing field for most people: you don't have to be physically gifted athletically to be successful. They have a story, they put you in charge. Autonomy, surely, is an aspect of happiness. Insecurity is to admit that you are not autonomous: something can be taken away from you.

Unfortunately, in this world so many live in a state of insecurity whether it be economic, emotional, psychological, sexual. The fight for civil rights has always been a fight for autonomy, a fight for one's capacity to pursue happiness in an equal manner to everyone else, a fight against insecurity in a way that challenges and changes cultural mores. The unfortunate aspect of such fights is that often can make others feel insecure. This is a problem in binary thinking: there's an us and them. Exist in nonduality and security is guaranteed. That's the notion behind one of the greatest sentences in American history: All men are created equal. Of course, the founding fathers were hampered by their era, but over the years this has come to mean all people are created equal.

I READ, TOO, PEANUTS COMICS, AND HAD ONE BOOK TITLED *HAPPINESS IS a Warm Puppy*: the cover featured Charlie Brown hugging Snoopy tightly. Linus always carried his security blanket. The parents, the teachers were never present; even when they were in the room, we didn't seem them or hear their voices. They were kids in search of some security, which is why Lucy offered Psychiatric advice for five cents; why Schroeder kept a bust of Beethoven on his piano: they sought authority or sought to portray authority, to make themselves a bit more grounded.

Despite her hectic schedule, my mother wasn't always absent: we spent time reading together many nights, and I've been fortunate to have had her be supportive of me, even when she disapproved of my choices. The insecurity of her absence was balanced by the security of those drives together, that reading time. Still, though, so much went unsaid, that secret became something that kept us from being closer. Keeping secrets became a practice I had to unlearn to be happy because in order to keep having secrets, I had to keep making new ones. And like the foundational one, it had be salacious.

When I taught in northern Michigan, I would invite visiting poets and fiction writers regularly to talk to my creative writing students, and one prominent novelist and short story writer suggested my students should know their characters by writing down their secrets. The idea being that people will do anything to keep a secret and many people will do anything to discover someone else's secrets. Keeping a secret means it's secure; being found out leads to insecurity, chaos, unhappiness.

Isn't this what Stevenson understood in his *Strange Case of Dr. Jeckyll and My Hyde*? Mr Hyde was hidden from the outside world though he thrived within Jeckyll. Even the name is deliberate: Hyde being all id, all what we bury in the name of polite society.

This is about masks. I learned to wear a mask early on and kept wearing ones, switching them out, and each time I hurt someone it wasn't the mask wearer but the mask who did it. I could switch it out, for my next "better" self. But every time the mask was exposed, I experienced rushes of panic, of instability, because my "happiness" was based on a faulty foundation, on protecting and maintaining secrets, those things that were the very source of insecurity in my life.

IN OTHER WORDS, MY GOAL REMAINED KEEPING WHATEVER SITUATIONAL MASK I wore smiling. It was only after I gave those up that I could start thinking about pursuing happiness.

ONE OF THE LAST THINGS MY FATHER SAID TO ME BEFORE WE STOPPED TALKING a few years back was that I was too sensitive. And I admit, through much of my adolescence and into my twenties, I was fairly sensitive: prone to take criticism to heart, empathetic to a fault, and lacking what some might call a killer instinct. I would rather laugh in competition and lose than win. For my father, who chose to play poker on Sundays at the club rather than see his kids, this was a sign of weakness, I am sure; some refutation of his values.

Yes, I was sensitive. I'd had power and strength used against me in ways that had demeaned me, so, of course, I spent much of my time, particularly as I came to terms with being a sexual creature, wary of my own strength and seeking approval in other ways: being a musician and a poet, deliberately casting myself against the typical forms of athletic strength my father valued.

By the time I hit my thirties and a father myself, I had come to terms with much of this, but still I was too sensitive for my father. By then, I'd defined myself as a parent by doing what I thought he wouldn't do. He wouldn't show up when promised, so I would show up earlier and do more, over-compensating at times. And still, my father once asked when I was a successful parent, professor, and poet when I was going to give up those gigs and use my talents where I could make some money, in advertising.

My father and I have different sets of values. We live in different communities. For over half my life I made peace with father-figures in my life, older poets and musicians and drummers who taught me things about music and art and teaching and women and whiskey. Whether it was playing basketball with Rich Silverman or poker with Stephen Dunn, I found "fathers" along the way for guidance. And still, I felt something missing. Until we stopped speaking, I'd tried different ways of forging a bond between my father and me. When I would see him those few times a year, he would say he wished we talked more, but he never called, he never reached out. When

I would drive the five hours to New York, he would ask me to get back in the car to come visit him in Brooklyn. When I pointed out to him that he was the parent when I was a child and so he established the relationship we had, I was too sensitive. I realized he saw me still as a fourteen-year-old.

My father never knew I was sexually assaulted, or if he does know, he never discussed it with me. Telling him would have required a place of intimacy that we did not share. For years I desired a relationship with my father. That desire came with chronic disappointment and fed my unhappiness. The behaviors that were most damaging in my life were my unconscious attempts to be more like him or at least more like I perceived him. Giving up my father meant giving up those behaviors, too. Giving up that desire meant re-establishing my values so I might find peace. And in peace, happiness.

I HAVE NO DOUBT THAT NICK WHO MOLESTED ME WAS UNHAPPY, WAS DRIVEN BY whatever insecurities he suffered. I don't mean this to justify what he did, nor do I mean to say I forgive him. My forgiveness has no place in his life and to say I did would be to seem braggartly, like I'm a better man. I'm not. I feel pity for the person he was then. I hope he found peace at some point later in life, if for no other reason than I don't want for him to have perpetuated a series of similar hurts on other kids.

I hope the people I've hurt along the way feel similarly about me. My indiscretions were many, made out of a combination of self-protection and self-sabotage. "I'm just a soul whose intentions are good…." but, of course, I was misunderstood, mostly by myself. I looked at what I wanted not at why I wanted. Desire that source of suffering. My own and of others.

Desire my long-time companion, like my shadow, disappearing at night or in the noonday sun, though at other times long and overreaching, and completely two-dimensional.

T HERE IS NO PATH TO HAPPINESS. HAPPINESS IS THE PATH."
So said the Buddha.

Aspire. Aspire. Aspire.

Shackleton died during a later attempt to get to the South Pole, a heart attack on South Georgia Island. He was an Antarctic explorer. It seems fitting: literally, he died on his path.

Like all paths, there may be brambles, there may be highwaymen, there may be roadblocks. More the path is yours alone and yet there will be companions along the way. You will get on board the bus for a bit and drive down the road. You will sing together. We will get on the ship and go on an expedition to the South Pole. We will be a community of pilgrims, explorers, each simultaneously alone together.

For years I thought I would find someone with whom I could be "happy together," but now I know my happiness is mine: I can choose to share it with others, but my happiness can't make them happy. To try to do so is both futile and self-serving. How often had I thought if I can make someone "happier" they will love me, and my insecurity will be sated. It never worked, any more than I someone loving me could make me happy. I looked for the places where they failed, chose to focus on what they didn't bring to the table rather than what they contributed. Or else I feared what others might say: that a partner wouldn't be _____ enough for acceptance because I was insecure in my friendships, my familial ties, my communities. "Of all forms of caution, caution in love is perhaps the most fatal to true happiness," said Bertrand Russell, and in my caution, I failed those communities, those partners, and myself.

More though, what's at issue is that I wasn't good enough, secure enough, grounded enough, _____ enough for these relationships. I looked for weaknesses in others to avoid the weakness in myself.

THE YORUBA OF NIGERIA SAY "NO ONE CAN LEAVE THEIR CHARACTER behind him when he goes on a journey." If happiness is the path, one has to make peace with that traveling companion over the course of the journey.

R EMEMBER TO STAY HUMBLE BEFORE THE PAGE," IS MY MANTRA when I write. I mentioned this to students once, and one said he couldn't imagine I was humble about anything. It got a laugh. But truth is, I ascribe to what the poet Lucille Clifton noted: "People wish to be poets more than they wish to write poetry and that's a mistake. One should wish to celebrate more than they wish to be celebrated."

No matter how successful a poem is it says nothing about the next one I have to write: I have to relearn the process of writing a poem, more I have to learn the process of writing that particular new poem: it's unique so I must pay attention to what the images and the languages seem to want to do. The same process will mean the same poem, just as any recipe followed will lead to the same meal. Process leads to discovery. Process is doing the work, and work is the great equalizer. I distrust anyone who says writing poems is easy.

Aspire aspire aspire.

I remain humble when I jack up the MG, pull out the socket set: I know doing something wrong can lead to disaster: a break down, an engine fire, an accident. I pay attention, have learned to double check each tightened bolt, each soldered connection. Ditto, I remain humble when I pick up the guitar, aware of my own shortcomings as a player. I pay attention to fingering, to my strumming. For this reason, I've brought a guitar and a small amp with me to practice here. Work is a practice. Practice is work. Call it attentiveness or call it mindfulness, doesn't matter: it's essential to working well. Working well is the one thing in my power.

I've not mastered humility. I've not mastered the guitar. I've not mastered poetry. I've not mastered teaching, I've not mastered parenting, I've not mastered loving, though I show up to do the work of them all, to be better. I've not mastered happiness, though I continue to be present, to continue to do the work.

I PLAY MUSIC BECAUSE IT BRINGS ME JOY. I PLAY MUSIC WITH A BAND because it forces me to be a part of a working community, each of us with jobs, each of us contributing, each collaborating to make something bigger than what we might do individually. We have our roles, and the sum of what we do is greater than each of us. I like the shared values of being in a band. We play punk rock, just loud, assertive rock n roll. Someone said I was too happy to play such angry music, and perhaps they're right, but the anger and insecurity and the hurt boy inside me continues to need a release.

We used to cover "We're a Happy Family" by the Ramones: the family's dysfunctional, fucked up, funny. In the Ramones, every member shared the surname Ramone to suggest brotherhood. My own family of musical outcasts in this western Maryland enclave has become part of a greater community, and we're happy even if "our troubles never end." We know we can overcome them together.

Punk rock instilled in me the importance of scene, of community. If everybody chips in (who books the bands, who publishes a zine, who finds a venue, who puts people up) the community thrives. People get the enjoyment of seeing bands play the music they like, maybe even some of them do it well. Scenes have a shared sense of values that have nothing to do with politics or religion or sexual orientation: they are about working together to make something bigger happen. This is a model for better communities in general, but it requires a sense of inclusiveness not exclusiveness. When I read about another African American killed by police I flinch because it emphasizes that the community at large sees Blacks as other, and it shows a side of the United States that is un-united, non-inclusive.

I've been the outsider, the misfit, the punk. I empathize with that sense of otherness.

THE *PARTRIDGE FAMILY* THEME ASKED US "TO COME ON GET HAPPY." The Beatles told us "Happiness is a warm gun." The Kinks assured us "Everybody's gonna be happy" while the Buzzcocks, ironically, let us know "Everybody's happy nowadays." Reagan Youth asked "Are you really happy?" The Replacements celebrated being unsatisfied. The Rolling Stones insisted "I can't get no, satisfaction."

Of course, I couldn't either. I didn't know what I needed to be satisfied, just another struggling human being. On *Exile on Main Street*, they declared, "I need a love to keep me happy," and I believed them. Unfortunately, I wasn't an attentive reader at that age because the key phrase there is "keep me," which implies that Mick Jagger is already happy. But even that philosophy of *needing* "a lover to keep me happy" is a lot of pressure on many of the relationships I've had. *My* happiness was dependent on *them*? For whatever good it does, I apologize to all my exes who couldn't live up to that monumental task. It wasn't their job—just like it isn't the job of my GrubHub driver to deliver my happiness on the coldest day of the year. He tried the best he could to get dinner here quickly. Those women tried to love me the best they could. I just didn't understand what their role was then. I failed them in not being able to keep them happy, too.

The editor in me now suggest that we say "happier" in such phrases. I'm happy. I need a lover to help make me happier. Why? It would add another vocation to my life, give me something to aspire to. Of course, that means seeing love not about something people do for us so much as what we do for each other. Aspiration. That's why so many times we fail, why so many times I couldn't "get no satisfaction." Like so many of us, I was busy looking at what I didn't have that I forgot to look at what was there, what had been satisfied. I wasn't keeping my PMA.

The Circle Jerks sang, "Be nice, say thank you, say please once in a while, /it's a beautiful world we live in, give your brother a smile." I remember, after a particularly bad break up singing that song, "Wonderful" ironically and loud down Broadway, pulling bus transfers from a packet of them I'd found and throwing them behind me as two friends followed, watching to ensure I wasn't arrested. 3 A.M. A few days after Christmas. The transfers were these strips of thin pink paper, and they flew off in the wind like giant confetti. One of those friends, Mark suggested maybe I would be happy in the new year, as if anguish vanishes when we buy a new calendar.

Mark died twenty years ago. The other friend I haven't spoken to in thirty. The self I was then is long gone, too. I remain grateful for both of them as they helped me get here. Gratitude is a cornerstone of keeping a positive mental attitude. I say thank you to those exes and friends who tried. I give them all a smile.

THE DALAI LAMA AND THICH NHAT HAHN AND SEVERAL OF MY TEACHERS have talked about the importance of smiling, how we are the only species that can smile, how it relaxes the face, how it sets the mood for those we interact with. There's even a book titled *Why is the Dalai Lama Always Smiling*. He has even declared that his practice, when he sees someone, is to smile. Consider a practice that is just to smile.

Psychologists note that smiles have important mental health benefits, and smiles provide an interesting chicken-egg conundrum. Do we smile because we feel good, or do we good because we smile? The answer is it doesn't matter: although a forced smile seems artificial and actually over-extends the facial muscles, learning how to smile can improve one's sense of positivity and help improve social interaction. Biochemistry stands behind this: when we smile, we release dopamine, endorphins, and serotonin into the bloodstream, all of which improve our mood.

Similarly, laughter, which I think of as a full-bodied smile, has proven to boost the immune system, relax muscles, and improve circulation. More importantly, thanks to an even bigger boost of dopamine, endorphins, and serotonin, it can lower anxiety, alleviate tension, and lift spirits. Being able to laugh, too, helps with one's resilience, particularly if one can laugh at one's self.

When my son was younger, we would listen to *Car Talk* on NPR, often just to hear Click and Clack the Tappet Brothers laugh. They let out belly roars, often at their own expense, and it reminded both Alex and me as to the importance of not taking things too seriously. My mother's Cousin Steve, who was like an uncle to me, laughed similarly: a barrel being opened.

So many people feel embarrassed about laughing too loud; they get self-conscious. What will people think? In their masks of ironic cool or good employee/student, wanting to laugh can create a moment of insecurity: *nobody else is laughing, oh no!* By giving yourself permission to laugh you reassert the security of your feelings. This was funny, and I laughed. In the last several years I've given myself permission to laugh fully when I find something funny. It is a kind of freedom that adds to the joy in my life. I don't think I am happier so I laugh and smile more; I think I am happy because I let myself smile and laugh more.

MUSIC IS ONE OF THOSE WELLS I CAN DIP INTO TO FIND JOY. When things seem particularly dark these days, I sing a chorus from the old punk band, X: "I must not think bad thoughts." Another mantra, it serves to remind me, that my thinking manufactures my reality. The world is perceived by me. It doesn't lessen the moments of despair so much as it reminds me that I have some control over the situation. Sadness, anguish, grief, disappointment, frustration, anger, rage: *I must not think bad thoughts.* They're there. They're a part of me. But they co-exist alongside joy, success, friendship, love, excitement.

Still, I dislike songs that feel trite: I never was a fan of "Don't Worry be Happy" because it failed to acknowledge that worry is something we do. Perhaps it's more essential "to worry but choose to be happy." More honest, but it doesn't make for a good melody. We can't not worry: the bills need to be paid, my brother has cancer, it's below zero and when I go to the car tomorrow it might not start because of the cold. Worry. But look beyond the worry: I have this room, a hard drive full of music, a belly full, now, of food. The aftertaste lingers in my mouth, reminds me of my good fortune.

Out the window, the cloud cover has gone, the snow, for now done, though, because its so frigid outside, a dusting of it blows sometimes with the wind, makes apparitional figures that swoop and sink back onto the courtyard. I don't know what the Inuit word for this is. Above, the moon wanes, some of its dark side exposed. I'm reminded it's called the dark side because it's unknown, it remains, thanks to tidal locking, on the far side from earth. Perhaps that's a metaphor.

Is the moon presenting a mask that hides its dark side the way we do? We have to acknowledge the dark side but somehow keep it so that we're tidal locked. This takes practice, a reminder that our dark side is with us but isn't us. Maybe that's why I like Sheryl Crow's song so much: "if it makes you happy, why are you so sad?"

Nonduality.

I CLEAN UP THE TABLE FROM DINNER, RETURN THE REST OF THE VINDALOO and rice to a plastic container; cover the rest of nan with foil; decide to eat the last of the pakora, one more dip into the mint chutney. I like the creamy green color, the cool runny texture, even as the pakora has wilted some since it was cooked. I pop it whole in my mouth: it still tastes delicious, and I'm mindful of this even as I go about the cleaning. The leftovers are a reminder of my abundance, and they will be in the refrigerator tomorrow should I want more.

I think of all the meals I've cooked: the time and work of preparation, the brevity of the dining, the time and work of cleaning up. There's work on both sides of satisfaction. Too many people resent the work not realizing the effort is where happiness happens. Our agency is in our labor and in our work ethic.

Tomorrow the temperature will remain under ten degrees, though the forecast suggests a warming trend into the teens shortly. I know better than to focus on what the temperature will be by the weekend. Tonight is what I have. These words on this page. This lingering taste.

Tomorrow my students and I will discuss the Jane Kenyon poem "Happiness," in which she writes:

> *No, happiness is the uncle you never*
> *knew about, who flies a single-engine plane*
> *onto the grassy landing strip, hitchhikes*
> *into town, and inquires at every door*
> *until he finds you asleep midafternoon*
> *as you so often are during the unmerciful*
> *hours of your despair.*

Happiness comes, I'm reminded, like a dinner ordered. It shows up on its schedule. It's almost always delicious. But it comes with hunger before it.

THERE IS NO DESSERT. ALTHOUGH I LIKE SWEETS, I DID NOT THINK TO ORDER dessert and I hadn't packed any treats for my nights here. I'm not hungry, but still, momentarily I feel a pang of frustration, of aggravation, of dissatisfaction, one that's completely manufactured by my mind. My appetite and my want for tastes has been satisfied. Is my desire for dessert cultural or personal? If I had no cultural concept of dessert, would I want something now? Probably not. Or is my own dissatisfaction? Do I want something more because my wants and needs have been met? In other words do I want for the sake of wanting? I remember John Stuart Mill, who taught "I have learned to seek my happiness by limiting my desires, rather than in attempting to satisfy them."

I can't argue the fact that I've had a delicious dinner. I have a warm room on a cold night. I have a stack of poetry collections, the internet, a computer full of songs and ways to reach out to my extended community of friends and family. That I *want* a piece of chocolate or a cookie right now is a superfluous desire. I will not suffer from hunger or disappointment without it. This is a desire without need and a desire without satisfaction. More, it seems to be ungrateful for everything I've just experienced: the spicy goat, the rice, the garlicky bread. I remember the joy of these things, think again of my craving and let it go.

I'm reminded sometimes I start a poem and write eight lines and it fails to go further even though I *want* it to. I let it go. Sometimes I draft a poem for eight weeks and even though it's a finished thing, it doesn't seem to work, and I think, maybe if I do a little more work…. But no, despite my desires for the poem it fails to be better than what it is, so I let it go, too. Not every poem started can be finished. Not every night can end with dessert or a kiss or shot of whiskey. I'm grateful that many have and many still will. Not tonight though.

In his poem "Gratitude," Cornelius Eady offers "to those/who defend poetry/against all foreign tongues:/Love." I think of Cornelius, one of those father figures in my life, my early poetry teacher, and think how if I weren't teaching these weeks, I would visit him for his birthday. Back when I was an undergraduate, I would see the light on in his apartment window on West Third Street across from Bleecker Bob's Records, and I would ring the buzzer and wait for the invitation for a drink and another conversation about poetry and music. What he taught me was love. What he taught me was gratitude. What he taught me was how to teach. I take these lessons to the page and to the classroom and to my daily interactions.

I go to my guitar, play around with some chords. B to C to D. E to A and back to B. Something seems to be working. I've trained myself so that my instincts can be trusted. That's what work is. I consider the Circle Jerks' "Wonderful" and think about the Bad Brains celebrating their PMA (Positive Mental Attitude): I want to write a positive punk manifesto. I'll call it "Gratitude." It'll take me three years to get it right, I'm sure. The work is the work.

Sometimes someone will say they're sorry about the way I was raised or what happened to me as a child, but it led me to the life I live. I'm grateful for the work of my mother and grateful for my father's absence that afforded me a level of freedom, and grateful to the modicum of privilege I've had. My mother taught me even if we have a little, we can give to others. To want others to be able to love freely, to have the same freedoms I have, to have their holidays honored is not a way of me having less so much as it a way of being grateful for the abundance we have by wanting others to have it to.

Tomorrow in class my students will work on poems of celebration.

Tomorrow I will have to leave for Carlow's campus, which means getting up early and into the cold, starting the car and letting it warm up. The forecast suggests that at 8:30 when I go to the parking lot it'll be about 0 degrees with a wind chill much lower than that. I know I will complain going to the car, and sit huddled, shaking in it, hoping the battery hasn't died overnight, while I put the key in the ignition. I will, no doubt, tell myself I am stupid for teaching right now, during my winter break. I will, no doubt, think about some vacation in a warm climate, the sound of waves hitting a beach. This moment in the car, the wind battering the window, will not be a moment of unhappiness but a moment of doubt, of frustration, of reaction.

Of course, it's only this second job that would allow me the opportunity for such a vacation.

Of course, if I were on a beach right now, drinking coffee while planning my day, I would no doubt be envying my friends teaching in low residency programs.

Of course, once the car starts, the heater will slowly warm up the cabin, my feet and fingers first, then slowly extending up the legs and arms. I will drive the few miles to campus I will forget all of those momentary thoughts. My poets will be waiting. My friends. We will talk about what we did the night before and I will tell my Indian food story. I will not doubt that teaching writing is my vocation that gets me out of bed and into a cold that feels almost hostile. I will consider Robert Hayden's famous poem, "Those Winter Sundays" about his father waking "in the blue-black cold" to make "banked fires blaze," and "love's austere and lonely offices," and remember how lucky I am to love my students and poetry and teaching and my friends who teach with me.

CARLOW IS A CATHOLIC UNIVERSITY. IT'S AMAZING HOW FAR I'VE COME FROM Catholic school, yet here I am again, a somewhat practicing Buddhist teaching poetry. When I was a teenager playing punk rock in New York, Pittsburgh was a demarcation line: as far as we were willing to go to play a show in a day, usually at the Electric Banana. Then, Pittsburgh was a dingy place, poster city for the rust belt and the end of a manufacturing middle class. The audiences were my sort of people: latchkey kids, loners, the haunted. Those without a community making a community.

The ghost of that city remains its street names and neighborhoods, in its working-class bars, and in the few remaining mills, but truly the city has reinvented itself. There's a brewery in an old church, now. There are lofts in old mills. Some of this is progress, but it's come at the devastation of livelihoods and a way of life. Nonduality.

I call my mother, and she talks about the my having come full circle. Outside is nightdark but snow falls again in tiny pellets filled with street light. Nonduality. The circle is full: it holds the yin and yang, I think.

I OPEN UP YOUTUBE, FIND K.C. AND THE SUNSHINE BAND. "CELEBRATE." I turn the volume up. Sure, there's a draft in the suite, but I don't care. I'm grateful. I'm happy. The way William Carlos Williams taught me, I strip down and dance. I've never been a good dancer, but dancing is a process: feel the beat, the rhythm, and try to let the body respond to it. I remain humble on the dance floor that is the living room of this suite in Pittsburgh. The duck watches. I don't care.

Is this happiness? It's as straight forward an answer as I can give.

About the Author

Gerry LaFemina's poetry collections include *Baby Steps in Doomsday Prepping*, *The Story of Ash* and *Little Heretic*. His essays on prosody, *Palpable Magic*, came out in 2015 and Kendall Hunt recently released his textbook, *Composing Poetry: A Guide to Writing Poems and Thinking Lyrically*. He teaches at Frostburg State University and in the Carlow University MFA Program. https://gerrylafemina.com/

GRATITUDE

I would like to thank Brandon Fury and Kara Knickerbocker for conversations that were the impetus for this book. To Mercedes for increasing my happiness pool. To my son, Alex, who reminds me every day to live in my joy. To my mom (Toni), Michael and Barbara, and Robin and Owen.

To Jennifer Browne and Reginald McKnight who read an early draft of this manuscript and whose insight and attention were invaluable to making this book happen.

To my good writer friends whose work inspires and whose companionship keeps me buoyed: George Guida, Jan Beatty, Dennis Hinrichsen, Stephen Dunn, Cornelius Eady, Michael Waters, Lynn McGee, Joy Gaines-Friedler, Madeleine Barnes, Bob Kunzinger, Rick Campbell, Gregg Wilhelm, Allison Joseph, Richard Peabody, Barbara Hurd, and Garret Keizer.

To my fellow members of The Downstrokes: Robin Summerfield, Greg Wood, Leigh Abraham, and Joe Jessen.

Extra special thanks to Frostburg State University for a sabbatical leave that allowed me to take the collected notes for this book and finish it. And to my colleagues and friends.

And to the Carlow University MFA community in both Pittsburgh and Dublin, for their support and the residency time that led to the writing of this book's first draft.

Thanks to Kim Davis and Madville Publishing for their support and belief in the work.

Lastly, thanks to all the musicians, bands, writers, and artists who have led me to questions and answers about happiness.

9 781948 692786